6th Edition

Educator's Internet
Companion

Christopher Mautner
Timothy McLain
Vince DiStefano
David Kershaw

classroom
CONNECT™

http://www.classroom.com

ACKNOWLEDGMENTS

Senior Editor	Chris Hofer
Revisions Editor	Kathleen M. Housley
Editor	Todd Frey
Creative Director	Heidi Lewis
Cover & Interior Design	Craig Matthews
Production	Audrey J. Singer
Manufacturing	Benjamin Cintas

CREDITS

CHAPTER 2: *White Pine Software,* p. 25: CU-SeeMe & Reflector information courtesy of White Pine Software; http://www.wpine.com.

CHAPTER 3: *AskERIC,* pp. 37–40: Educational Resources and Information Center; http://ericir.syr.edu; AskERIC is funded by the U.S. Dept. of Transportation.

CHAPTER 4: *Concertina Children's Books,* p. 85: http://www.iatech.com/books/intro.htm; © 1994 by Sharon Katz; all rights reserved. *Educational Resources and Information Center,* p. 89: http://ericir.syr.edu; AskERIC is funded by the U.S. Dept. of Transportation. *EdWeb,* p. 90: http://edweb.gsn.org/; Exploring Technology and School Reform, by Andy Carvin; all rights reserved. *Grand Canyon National Park,* p. 94: http://www.kaibab.org/; © 1997 Bob Ribokas, all rights reserved; this publication and its text and photos may not be copied for commercial use without the express written permission of Bob Ribokas, ribokas.bob@teradyne.com. *Family Health,* p. 94: The Family Health Web site is maintained at the Ohio University Telecommunications Center and is a service of the Telecommunications Center and the College of Osteopathic Medicine at Ohio University; http://www.fhradio.org.

CHAPTER 5: *Yahoo!,* pp. 120, 125: http://www.yahoo.com; text and artwork © 1997 by Yahoo!, Inc.; all rights reserved. *Yahooligans!,* p. 126: http://www.yahooligans.com/; text and artwork © 1996 by Yahoo!, Inc.; all rights reserved; Yahoo! and the Yahoo! logo are trademarks of Yahoo!, Inc. *Lycos,* p. 135, and *LycosTop 5%,* p. 123; http://www.lycos.com; © 1994-1997 Carnegie Mellon University; all rights reserved; Lycos is a registered trademark of Carnegie Mellon University; used by permission. *Magellan Internet Guide,* p. 124, (http://www.mckinley.com/) and *Excite,* p. 132, (http://www.excite.com/Info/): Excite, Excite Search, and the Excite Logo are trademarks of Excite, Inc. and may be registered in various jurisdictions. Magellan Internet Guide and the Magellan logo are trademarks of The McKinley Group, Inc. a subsidiary of Excite, Inc., and may be registered in various jurisdictions. Excite screen display © 1995–1997 Excite, Inc. Magellan screen display © 1997 The McKinley Group, Inc., a subsidiary of Excite, Inc. *AltaVista,* pp. 128–130: http://www.altavista.digital.com; AltaVista images with permission from Digital Equipment Corporation; © 1997 Digital Equipment Corporation; all rights reserved. *Infoseek:* p. 134 http://www.infoseek.com; reprinted by permission; Infoseek, Ultrasmart, Ultraseek, iSeek, Quickseek, Imageseek, Ultrashop, "proof of intelligent life on the net," once you know you know and the Infoseek logos are trademarks of Infoseek Corporation, which may be registered in certain jurisdictions; other trademarks shown are trademarks of their respective owners; © 1995–1997 Infoseek Corporation; all rights reserved. *HotBot,* p. 133: http://www.hotbot.com; HotBot images with permission from Wired Digital, Inc.; © 1994–97 Wired Digital, Inc.; all rights reserved. *WebCrawler,* p. 138: http://www.webcrawler.com; screen captures from MetaCrawler with permission from go2net, Inc.; © 1997 go2net, Inc.; all rights reserved.

Due to the changing nature of the Internet, site addresses and their content may vary. Great care has been used in choosing the very best of the Web for inclusion in this book, but no long-term assurances can be made regarding their suitability for school use.

All terms mentioned in this book that are known to be trademarks or service marks have been appropriately capitalized.

Classroom Connect, Inc.

Corporate Office
1241 East Hillsdale Boulevard
Foster City, California 94404

http://www.classroom.com

ISBN: 0-932577-10-5

Printed in the United States of America.

2 3 4 5 6 7 8 9 10 . 02 01 00 99

Table of Contents

An Introduction to the Internet

The Internet is one of the fastest growing communications media in history. Don't believe it? Consider some of these Net statistics:

- As of June 1999, 92 million Americans and Canadians - or 40% of the population over the age of 16, report they use the Internet, according to the 1999 CommerceNet/Nielsen Media Research study.
- At least 160 countries are connected to the Internet.
- In the fall of 1998, 89 percent of U.S. public schools had access to the Internet.
- Eighty-seven percent of public schools that did not have access to the Internet had plans to obtain access by the year 2000. Thus, 95 percent of the nation's public schools were expecting to obtain Internet access by the end of the century.

Many leading K-12 schools are part of this explosive online growth. Why? Because schools that use the Internet do not simply bring children into the future of information technology. They turn their students into something education reformers have been talking about for years — lifelong learners.

Teachers who work the Internet into their curricula — not for its own sake, but to teach students how to use the network to find and use information to reach a goal — turn students into independent thinkers and learners, rather than rapt, or not so rapt, listeners.

Starting the Revolution Without Schools?

Whatever the Internet is, it's certainly not a fad. And the 105,544 public and private K-12 schools in the United States cannot afford to be left behind during this technological revolution. Evidence of a growing separation of our society into technological haves and have-nots requires that children of all backgrounds have access to an information technology that is sweeping through all levels of government, business, and education.

Is the Internet really that persuasive? Yes, and more so every day. The Supreme Court, NASA, the White House, the Smithsonian Institution, Congress, and the United Nations have all gone online to make archives of information available to *anyone* — not just reporters, researchers, or people with the time to travel to Washington, D.C., or New York City. Your local library, city hall, and county government will undoubtedly be next, if they aren't already online.

More and more businesses are opening up shop on the Internet every day. The Cable News Network, flower shops, car dealers, bookstores, real estate brokers, and travel agents are just a few examples. And since the Internet has its roots in research institutions, many colleges and universities have been online for more than two decades.

States and Schools Push to Get Online

More states are recognizing that their K-12 schools need access to the Information Superhighway. Some are wiring every new school building with fiber optics, simplifying educators' often daunting problem of finding the phone lines to get onto the Internet. Other states are appropriating money for schools to acquire the phone lines they need. Even the Federal government is getting involved through the development of programs like Goals 2000.

http://www.ed.gov/G2K/

More often than not though, schools are not waiting for the education bureaucracy to bring the fast-developing Internet to them. Technology committees made up of parents and educators are meeting to write proposals for grant money to wire their schools. Successful proposals bring in tens of thousands of dollars.

Internet "missionaries" such as computer teachers, library/media specialists, principals, or technologically oriented parents can be found in many schools. They round up a few volunteers, some computer hardware, and patch in a phone line just to get things started. Some schools even roll a computer from classroom to classroom on a cart and plug the phone line into the wall to get students online. Grassroots events like NetDay further this community involvement by having volunteers from local companies, parents, and other citizens donate computer equipment to help get their school districts wired. The new E-Rate also promises to help schools pay for online technology.

http://netday.org

http://www.E-Rate.net

Teachers Take Students Around the World

What do educators do with the Internet after they've met the challenges of setting it up? Besides teaching students to search for, find, and use information, they bring students into contact with people they would never have otherwise met. While the Net is comprised of mountains of information, it's also made of people of all races, creeds, cultures, and colors — and they all have personal stories and knowledge to share. Because the culture of the Internet is based on free sharing of information, busy professionals, renowned experts worldwide, and countless others dispense their knowledge with no expectation of payment, except perhaps thanks. That is a worthwhile lesson in itself for young people.

With the Internet, teachers can make class and individual student projects global affairs. Teachers match students with email penpals anywhere in the world to collect weather data, to learn about world cultures, or to practice Spanish with native speakers. Students can join a global project to correspond with explorers in the Arctic or Central American jungles. They can invite a scientist or writer to visit them electronically to exchange questions and answers. The possibilities are limitless. The challenge for teachers is to somehow structure this huge and exciting resource into their students' everyday classroom lives.

How Classroom Connect

and This Book Help Educators

This book and other Classroom Connect products help educators bring the Internet directly to their students. Few educators have the time to simply wander around the Internet and find what is valuable to them. Classroom Connect's sole goal is to keep teachers abreast of new educational Internet resources and help them apply these resources in the K-12 classroom. The *Educator's Internet Companion* shows educators and students where to go on the Net to find the resources and information they need. More importantly, this book helps teachers take this knowledge into the classroom and work it into lesson plans.

ORIGINS AND OVERVIEW

It's hard to define the Internet in a few sentences. Technically, the Net is an interconnecting, spiderweb-like system of millions of computer networks linked via telecommunications software and hardware.

To the people who use it, the Internet is really the sum of all individuals and institutions who connect their computers to other computers anywhere in the world with devices called modems. A computer with a modem can plug into any phone line, and that simple connection is enough to send people and information around the world via the Internet.

The wonderful thing about the Internet is that each computer on the network is considered equal — no one computer runs the whole show. An aging, clunky five-year-old Macintosh in your classroom is equal to a network of computers at NASA in the sense that both of them have access to the same information on the Internet. No person, government, organization, or business owns or operates the Internet. It is a truly democratic community.

Who Built the "Information Superhighway"?

The U.S. military laid the foundation in the early 1960s as a global, fail-safe communications network designed to operate even if one or more links became inoperative. Universities and research laboratories were granted access to the Internet as they began to do more direct business with the government. Funded mostly by federal money, the Internet was used exclusively by the government, research institutions, and colleges and universities for two decades.

But in 1992, policies regulating commercial use of the Internet were relaxed, allowing unrestricted use for commercial purposes. Now, commercial and nonacademic traffic has all but overwhelmed the Internet, and the U.S. Government has more or less backed away from subsidizing the network, although they do still fund research and academic work done by federal and educational institutions.

Within a year of the policy change, dozens of entrepreneurs formed companies offering low-cost Internet access to individuals and businesses. These companies came to be known as **Internet Service Providers,** or **ISPs.** The invention of the World Wide Web added to the excitement, as it not only brought graphics to the online community, but made using the Net as simple as pointing and clicking with a mouse.

Business people discovered that the Internet holds rich resources for research, public relations, marketing, customer service, and retail sales, and started a stampede for the online market that has yet to abate.

The Internet Community

According to recent estimates, more than 100 million people are online, while approximately 65 percent of all elementary and secondary schools in the United States are connected. Thousands of new Internet services and information locations come online each month. Best of all, almost all of these resources — including documents, software, and databases — are *free*, due in large part to the Internet's culture of sharing information and helping people solve problems.

The operational philosophy of the Internet is that of sharing information. Virtually all of the universities, libraries, schools, government agencies, and even most businesses online allow users to access their information at no cost. Likewise, individuals give advice and information expecting nothing but thanks in return. The battle cry of the Internet community is "Information wants to be free!" While this is changing as more and more "pay-per-use" commercial services spring up, many new users still experience an almost giddy feeling of camaraderie when they become part of this enormous yet personal global community.

Netiquette: the Online Rules of the Road

With all this frenzy of global activity, some kind of order is needed. While organizations like the Internet Society and InterNIC do play key roles in the Net's continuing development, there is no real Internet police force to patrol the inhabitants of the Net, per se. The lack of established rules has brought about the evolution of an informal code of conduct called *netiquette*.

For the most part, the atmosphere on the Net is congenial and open. But the very anonymity of electronic communication requires that each user must be aware of the personal responsibility that comes along with the privilege of having access to this treasure trove of information. Users who violate netiquette with thoughtless or inappropriate behavior are often *flamed* by angry users. That is, they quickly receive dozens or even hundreds or thousands of nasty email reprimands clogging their mailboxes as punishment.

Realize that what users access or send over the Internet directly affects other computer networks and their system administrators. Many of the rules of the Net have to do with the amount and kind of data that's transferred across thousands of networks. Computers and networks can only handle so much traffic, which is one of the reasons users consider the sending of "junk mail" over the Internet a violation of netiquette.

To make sure every user is aware of such issues, each computer network on the Internet has its own set of rules that users must follow while on the system. System operators could take away a user's "right" to access their resources if the user repeatedly violates their rules. Most policies forbid putting unlawful materials, like pirated software, on a system. They also ban abusive language or behavior, also known as *flame baiting* (an example of this would be posting crude racial comments). Transmitting messages that are designed to slow down or incapacitate another's computer/network is also prohibited.

Beyond these basic tenets, there is also a particular netiquette for using specific tools like email and Usenet newsgroups. We'll cover those later.

The Ten Commandments for Computer Ethics

1. Thou shalt not use a computer to harm other people.
2. Thou shalt not interfere with other people's computer work.
3. Thou shalt not snoop around in other people's files.
4. Thou shalt not use a computer to steal.
5. Thou shalt not use a computer to bear false witness.
6. Thou shalt not use or copy software for which you have not paid.
7. Thou shalt not use other people's computer resources without authorization.
8. Thou shalt not appropriate other people's intellectual output.
9. Thou shalt think about the social consequences of the program you write.
10. Thou shalt use a computer in ways that show consideration and respect.

(Source: The Computer Ethics Institute)

To sum up, here are the main rules of Netiquette that you should always keep in mind:

- Treat other online users as you would like to be treated.
- Be forgiving of other users' mistakes online; you were once (or are) an Internet "newbie" too!
- Know where you are in cyberspace at all times; what may be appropriate in one place online may be strictly forbidden in another.
- Lurk before you leap. Read what others have written before you post your own comments.
- Share your knowledge with others. When you learn something new, pass it along to someone else who can benefit.
- Respect other people's privacy; don't snoop around where you don't belong.

Getting Connected to the Net

Your school district may have already provided you and your students with a computer and a connection to the Internet. But in case they haven't, or in case you want to know how to access the Net from your home, the following information can help you make an informed decision on how best to join the online community. The good news is that new, user-friendly Internet browser software like Netscape Navigator and Microsoft's Internet Explorer and lower online access costs have made it easier and cheaper than ever before to surf the Net .

Going online doesn't have to be expensive. Your total online costs for one year most likely will be less than $300. If you already have a computer, all you'll need is:

- A modem, which connects your PC to a phone line. The current standard model is the 33.6, which costs about $75. If you are buying a modem for the first time and your local Internet Service Provider has 56K available, you could also purchase a 56K modem, which is considerably faster than the 33.6. With inexpensive cable modems and high-speed digital phone lines available in the very near future, however, the technology isn't necessarily worth the gamble or the money (usually about $100).

- A telephone line (about $14 to $20 per month).
- A subscription to a commercial online service or a direct Internet account with a local Internet Service Provider (ISP). Commercial services cost about $10 per month, with a $2 per hour usage charge. A local ISP will charge about $15 to $30 per month for unlimited, direct Internet access.

If you need to buy a computer, the price of an IBM-compatible Pentium, with a 75-megahertz processor and 540-megabyte hard disk drive (minimal configuration) is less than $1,400, including a high resolution color monitor and a modem. Complete Power Macintosh computer systems are now in the $1,300 range as well and are used by millions of Internet surfers every day.

Commercial Services

You can get connected to the Internet in two ways:

1. Via a commercial online service.
2. Direct Internet access through an Internet Service Provider (ISP).

Commercial services are big companies that pay to have other companies such as *Time* magazine and the *New York Times* put content within their virtual community. That's why they charge you a fee to access their information every month.

America Online (AOL), Prodigy, and the Microsoft Network are three popular commercial services. At a base level, commercial services let you connect to the online communities they've created and send email over the Internet. Beyond these basic offerings, most of them also allow you to surf the Net (albeit slowly).

Almost all the commercial services have extensive news and information that they receive from companies they have agreements with (magazines, newspapers, dictionary and encyclopedia companies, entertainment companies, etc.). Most of the information from commercial services is included in a flat monthly fee, but some have additional hourly costs.

If you decide to use commercial services instead of an Internet Service Provider (ISP), contact them at the addresses listed below. They'll be glad to provide you with the free software you'll need to connect to them. Often they'll waive the first month's fee or give you 10 or 15 free hours of connect time to get you started.

America Online

(800) 827-6364
URL: http://www.aol.com

Microsoft Network

(800) 386-5550
URL: http://www.msn.com

Prodigy

(800) PRODIGY
URL: http://www.prodigy.com

Internet Service Providers

All Internet Service Providers (ISPs) connect you directly to the Internet. There are no extra services like the commercial services provide, but typically there are also no hourly charges either.

ISPs usually charge a flat monthly fee, regardless of how long you spend on the Internet. For a small monthly fee, you can surf the Net to your heart's content and not rack up any hourly fees, making it the most cost-effective way to go.

Keep in mind that most ISPs provide really fast connections to the Net. That means you can surf the Net more efficiently and find the information you need in much less time than if you did it through a commercial service. ISPs usually provide the software you'll need to do basic email and Internet browsing too. Be sure to ask what software they provide. Think twice before signing up with an ISP that doesn't give you Netscape or Internet Explorer, or that won't tell you how to get it once you join.

Some Internet Service Providers are well-run companies, dedicated to providing users with quality service. They ensure that you will always be able to connect, and they have support personnel who will help you. Other ISPs may provide little or no support, and you may get a busy signal when you try to connect, especially during their prime times.

Before you choose an ISP, it might be prudent to talk to some of their current customers to find out what their experiences have been. In fact, don't pay an ISP for Internet service until you've asked a few colleagues and friends about their experiences on the Net.

Finding Internet Service Providers (ISPs)

You can keep long distance charges low by locating an ISP in your local calling area or by choosing one that offers low-cost, dial-up access through a local phone number. Call a few local computer stores to track down the phone numbers of local ISPs, or look in the Yellow Pages under Internet.

If you can't find a local ISP, don't despair. Below is a list of companies that can provide connections to the Internet anywhere in the United States. Their fees vary, so give them a call and ask for the best deal on a graphical (SLIP/PPP) Internet connection via a local phone number in your area.

AT&T WorldNet Services

(800) WORLDNET
URL: http://www.att.net

EarthLink Network

(800) 395-8425
URL: http://www.earthlink.net

HoloNet

(510) 704-0160
URL: http://www.holonet.net

IBM Global Network

(800) 775-5808

URL: http://www.ibm.com/globalnetwork/

MCI

(800) 550-0927

URL: http://www.mci2000.com

Mindspring

(800) 719-4660

URL: http://www.mindspring.com

NetCom

(800) 353-6600

URL: http://www.netcom.com

PSI (Performance Systems International)

(800) 82-PSI-82

URL: http://www.psi.com

Portal Information Network

(800) 433-6444

URL: http://www.portal.com

Verio Northeast

(888) getverio

URL: http://www.verio.net

Lists of ISPs on the Net

If you're already on the Internet and would like to look up ISP listings, visit these Web sites below.

Celestin

URL: http://www.celestin.com

Cyberspace Today ISP Index

URL: http://www.cybertoday.com/cybertoday/ISPs/ispinfo.html

ISP Finder

URL: http://ispfinder.com

The LIST

URL: http://www.thelist.com

Network USA ISP Catalog

URL: http://www.netusa.net/ISP

thedirectory

URL: http://www.thedirectory.org

All things considered, it's best to go with an ISP rather than a commercial service. ISPs are cheaper, faster, and give you better access to the Internet. Commercial services do provide specially designed content, but most of this content can just as easily be found via the World Wide Web, making the extra content superfluous.

A Word on Addresses in This Book

Before setting out on the Information Superhighway, it's helpful to understand how the "addresses" on the Internet operate. As important as understanding a street address is in the "real world," it is even more crucial in the "virtual world," so that users can be able to access Net computers and reach other users.

A quick aside: How do Web browsers know where to find WWW resources? They work on the basis of **Uniform Resource Locators,** called **URLs** for short. URLs are what the Web uses to indicate the location of information on the Internet. In essence, it's possible to represent almost any file or computer on the internet using a URL.

A URL consists of three parts. The first part is simply the letters URL, which tell you that this is, in fact, an Internet address. (**Note:** Never type the letters URL: when entering an address into your computer. Instead just type in everything that follows after the colon.) The second part is the URL prefix and shows the access method. In the Classroom Connect address, **URL: http://www.classroom.com,** the URL prefix **http://** tells you it is a Web site.

The third part of the URL gives the specific address for that particular site on the World Wide Web. It consists of a root address, which in this case is **www.classroom.com.** Sometimes the root address is followed by information that points to a specific subdirectory or filename. Those names are separated by forward slashes.

Here's an example of an actual subdirectory or filename added to the Classroom Connect Web address: **www.classroom.com/classroom/search.htm.**

The **classroom** part is the subdirectory, and **search.htm** is the name of the file in the **classroom** subdirectory containing the Web page about searching the Internet.

Note that a URL is always in the form of a single unbroken line containing no spaces.

Here are examples of URLs that can be accessed with a WWW browser:

http://www.eff.org

This URL connects you to the Electronic Frontier Foundation's Web server. (The **http://** prefix means this is a Web site.)

telnet://pac.carl.org

Opens a telnet or interactive session with this computer.

mailto:user@computer.edu

Opens an email message to this Internet user.

news:alt.hypertext

Allows you to read and send posts to this Usenet newsgroup.

Thus, URLs not only connect to other documents on the Web, but provide the ability to use other Internet services as well.

A Word About the Accuracy of Internet Addresses

The Internet is always evolving. In fact, change is the only certainty on this worldwide "network of networks." We have verified the accuracy of addresses as close to press time as possible, but some addresses could change after publication.

Take these steps if an address does not work:

- Check and retype the address.
- If you receive a message telling you the site has moved supplying you with its new address, which is much like the post office notifying you of an address change, copy the new address or add it to your bookmarks. Then try it. It should take you where you want to go.
- If you don't receive a message and if you typed the correct address, try stripping the address down to what is called the "root directory" and access. (This only works for Web sites.) For example, in the following address for WebElements, you would delete everything after the **edu** to reach the root directory, or the file where the Web site information resides.

    URL: http://www.cchem.berkeley.edu/Table/index.html

- If this doesn't work, go to the Classroom Connect Web site and use one of the six searching tools on the Search page to find your site on the Web.

    URL: http://www.classroom.com/classroom/search.htm

We'll talk about Internet addresses a little more in depth in the next chapter, Internet Tutorials.

HOW TO USE INTERNET NAVIGATION TOOLS

More than 100 million Internet users communicate with people in more than 160 countries, search through and retrieve information, and simply browse the global network of computers by using software commonly referred to as "navigation tools." These tools include email, Usenet newsgroups, and the World Wide Web. This chapter will give you brief tutorials on how to use these Internet essentials and will suggest ways to use them effectively in the classroom, including pointers to related resources. If you need help understanding the terms we use, consult the glossary at the end of the book.

Software used by personal computers to access the Internet is developing rapidly. Newly developed and inexpensive graphical software is available for both Windows and Macintosh computers. This software provides an easy-to-use, graphical, point-and-click interface to all the resources on the Internet.

World Wide Web

Since its beginnings in 1992, the World Wide Web has become the fastest growing and most exciting component of the Internet. That's because it allows Net surfers to use their mouse to point-and-click their way through the Internet's text, graphics, sounds, and video clips — which, thanks to the Web, can all be viewed on the screen at the same time.

The Web consists of millions of "pages" or screens of text and graphics that have built-in links (known as hyperlinks) to other pages on the Internet. To navigate the Web for information, you need **Internet browser** software that allows you to basically surf your way through tons of information and multimedia materials. Netscape Navigator and Microsoft's Internet Explorer are by far the most popular and powerful of these browsers.

Current versions of these browsers allow you to read Usenet newsgroups, send and receive email, and even create Web pages of your own. For students and educators, this means that the only Internet navigation software you may ever need for your computer is a copy of Netscape or Internet Explorer.

How to Get a Web Browser

When you sign up for Internet access, your Internet service provider will send you one of the following browsers on disk or CD-ROM. When your school is connected to the Internet, most often a browser is included in the set-up, too. To get the latest copy of either Internet browser, use one of the addresses listed below.

Netscape Navigator/Communicator

http://home.netscape.com

Microsoft Internet Explorer

http://www.microsoft.com/ie/

Web Addresses

Web pages, like other online sites and materials, have their own type of Internet address. Here's an example using the U.S. White House's Web address, and what that homepage looks like on the Internet.

http://www.whitehouse.gov

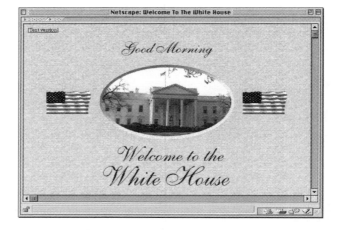

The **http://** portion of the White House Web address stands for something called **hypertext transmission protocol,** the method by which Web pages are transmitted over the Internet. All Web pages — which are really just files stored on an Internet server's hard drive — have these letters in front of their online addresses. So whenever you see an online address starting with **http://** you know it's a Web site.

The Web gets its name from the fact that Web pages and computers are interconnected in spiderweb-like fashion by **hypertext** and **hyperlinks,** which are simply words or pictures (icons) within a page that you can click on to instantly travel to some other Web document. It doesn't matter where on the Net the computer is located, and you don't have to *know* the address. Just point and click with your mouse, and your software does the rest.

Educational resources abound on the Web. You can find complete, hyperlinked texts of classic novels; short video clips of physics projects; dozens of museums, like the Louvre; sound clips of works by Mozart; detailed graphics of insects; even sites from other K-12 schools. With the Web you can pay a virtual visit to the White House or tour other nations. These are only a few of the sites educators and students can visit. (See Chapter 3, World Wide Web Tours, for some great places you can take your students.)

Students from hundreds of schools are learning how to create and mount their own Web pages — an easier task than many would imagine. In doing this they command a global audience for their projects, school newspapers, and other work. Creating Web pages requires HTML, Hypertext Markup Language. Learning HTML isn't difficult, and a variety of new HTML authoring software on the market makes it easier than ever to make a jaw-dropping, eye-catching Web site.

As you can imagine, the great thing about the Web is its multimedia capabilities. Full-color graphics, video, and sound clips are just as easy to access as text. And, like other Internet tools, the Web is entirely searchable. Users can enter the address for or link to numerous locations to begin keyword searches.

When you find something interesting or valuable, you can save it to a disk or hard drive, print it, or make a **bookmark** entry for the site. With millions of Web pages on the Internet, you'll use this feature a lot to find your way back to the things you've found!

Helpful Starting Points on the Web

Entering the World Wide Web: A Guide to Cyberspace
http://www.hcc.hawaii.edu/guide/www.guide.html

Starting Points for Web Navigation
http://www.ncsa.uiuc.edu/SDG/Software/Mosaic/StartingPoints/NetworkStartingPoints.html

The World Wide Web Consortium
http://www.w3.org

World Wide Web Frequently Asked Questions (FAQ) File
http://sunsite.unc.edu/boutell/faq/wwwfaq.txt

Yahoo! Internet Life: Surf School
http://www.zdnet.com/yil/filters/surfjump.html

Email

Email, or electronic mail, is by far the most widely used online tool. Virtually every Internet user gets started online by experimenting with electronic mail. Email is a valuable communication tool for numerous reasons:

- Unlike postal or "snail mail," email messages can be delivered at any time, regardless of carrier services, holidays, or weekends.
- Incoming messages can be immediately saved to a disk, printed, forwarded, or deleted.
- Outgoing messages can be carefully composed offline, delivered instantly, and even sent at specific times via software timers.
- An email message — unlike a telephone call — can be delivered independent of time zones, without long distance charges.
- Messages can be sent out to dozens, even thousands of people at once.
- Many users soon discover that they can eliminate annoying and time-wasting problems such as "telephone tag" and bad faxes.
- Millions of users who aren't even "on the Internet" can send and receive email. Anybody with an account to a commercial service like America Online or anyone with access to one of the thousands of local bulletin boards or networks with email gateways is a potential recipient of an email message.

As an education tool, however, email is invaluable. With a little creativity, students and teachers can instantly visit people and places all over the globe. Classes can communicate and participate in projects with students and educators in other nations, send questions to scientists in California, or ask the president about his foreign policy. Thousands of students already use email to share school information, practice foreign languages, exchange school newspapers, and learn about distant cities, cultures, and climates.

Email Addresses

Almost everyone on the Internet has an email address. Chances are that when you begin navigating the Net and making friends using email, your electronic mailbox will begin to fill up. Here's a hypothetical example of a standard email address:

llane@smallville.highschool.edu

Email addresses are always divided by the @ symbol, so this address would be read aloud as "llane at smallville dot highschool dot edu." The first part of the email address — the **llane** part — is called the user name. Most of the time, users get to pick their user names — but not always. In this case, Ms. Lane shortened her real name from Lucy Lane to just "llane" for her email address. If you get your email from certain commercial services, for example, you may be automatically assigned a screen name or number combination.

The part following the @ sign, **smallville.highschool.edu,** is the actual domain name, referring to the Internet domain where she receives her email. Domains are the names of Internet computers in the schools, businesses, and other organizations and institutions on the Net. Each computer has a unique domain name. The fictitious Smallville High School is **smallville.highschool.edu;** the real-world Cornell University is **cornell.edu;** the U.S. Navy is **navy.mil;** FidoNet is **fidonet.org;** and Apple Computer is **apple.com.**

Notice that the rightmost parts of the preceding domain names are different. In the United States, the three letters after the last period signify various types of entities — educational, commercial, military, nonprofit, or some other type of organization.

Common Domains on the Internet

Domain	Type
.com	Commercial
.edu	Educational
.gov	Governmental
.int	International
.mil	Military
.net	Internet Resource
.org	Nonprofit Organization

Sometimes you'll encounter other suffixes — two-letter extensions after the organizational extensions. These usually represent national domains: .au for Australia; .ca for Canada; .de for Germany; .fr for France; and .uk for the United Kingdom. So if an address reads **kkline@ting.umad.de** the ".de" indicates that this person sent a message from a computer in Germany. If there is no country extension to an address, assume the user is in the United States.

International Domains on the Internet

Domain	Country
.au	Australia
.ca	Canada
.ch	Switzerland
.de	Germany
.dk	Denmark
.es	Spain
.fr	France
.il	Israel
.it	Italy
.jp	Japan
.mx	Mexico
.nz	New Zealand
.pl	Poland
.ru	Russia
.tr	Turkey
.uk	United Kingdom
.us	United States
.va	Vatican

Unlike the postal service, the Internet system won't deliver mail with an almost perfect address. So, when sending email, be sure to type the recipient's complete email address with no mistakes. Otherwise, the message will bounce and be returned with a message saying the user is unknown. Most email addresses are case insensitive, meaning that it doesn't matter whether you type in upper or lower case. Experts advise, however, that you type an address exactly as it appears.

Sending an Email Message

Sending someone a message using an email program is as simple as filling in some basic **header** information and writing the actual message. Fill in the following to send an email message:

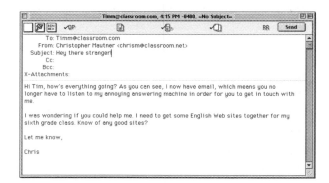

1. The To: field, where you place the recipient's address; that is, the person to whom you want to send the message.
2. The From: field, where you place your own address so the recipient can send you a message in return (most email programs do this automatically).

3. The Subject: line should contain a brief description of the message.

4. Put other online users' email addresses in the Cc: or carbon copy field to send them a copy.

5. The Attach feature is where you can indicate which files you want to send along with the message, if any. This feature allows you to piggy-back word processor files, graphics, sounds, etc. to your email.

6. Type your message in the message body, then send it on its way!

While using Internet Explorer or Netscape Navigator, when you come across an email address of someone you want to send email to, enter it into your browser in this fashion.

mailto:johndoe@internet.edu

By putting **mailto:** in front of the email address in your browser, a blank email message will automatically appear and allow you to fill it out and send it on its way.

Email Attachments

Although a majority of the messages transmitted around the Internet consist of text, email messages can actually take several forms. With today's advanced email software, you can transmit graphics, sound, and even video to other schools and students. These multimedia files, when sent along with (or "piggy-backed" to) an email message, are known as *attachments*.

Such technology makes the learning potential of email even more powerful. Students can exchange computer images of themselves with a class in Europe. Art students can send computerized works back and forth for critiques. School newspaper or yearbook editors can exchange desktop files and evaluate each others' work. Teachers can share lesson plans, Web sites they've found useful, and overhead slides. The possibilities are endless.

You can attach both *text* and *binary* files to your email messages. Text files include anything you've created in a word processor and then saved in what's called plain ASCII text. You can usually tell if something is a text file by its **.txt** extension. Binary files include all sorts of things like sound and video clips, graphics, HyperStudio stacks, and software programs of any kind or size. In reality, anything you can store on your hard drive can be attached to an email message.

Keep in mind that for attachments to work, you must send the attached file to someone who has a similar computer and software as you have. Sending your friends a Macintosh program won't do them any good if they have a Windows PC computer. They also won't be able to view a .gif (graphic) file you've sent if they don't have a program that can open those images. The bottom line is that the recipient of your attachments must have the same type of computer or program to be able to use any files you send.

Email Netiquette

Certain rules of netiquette apply to email, and it's important to be familiar with them. Email is easily stored and forwarded, so be professional and careful about what you say about others. Never assume your email is private, and never send anything that you would not mind seeing on the evening news.

Use discretion when forwarding mail to group addresses or distribution lists. It is considered extremely rude to forward personal email to mailing lists or Usenet newsgroups without the original author's permission.

Cite all quotes, references, and sources. It's preferable to reference the source of a document and provide instructions on how to obtain a copy. Respect copyright and license agreements. Don't use academic networks for commercial work.

When writing messages, keep paragraphs and messages short and to the point. Focus on one subject per message. Follow chain of command procedures for corresponding with superiors. Don't send a complaint via email directly to the top just because you can. Check your email daily — Internet users appreciate a quick reply. Email can pile up quickly and take up large amounts of disk space, so delete unwanted messages immediately.

When quoting another person, edit out whatever isn't directly applicable to your reply. Including irrelevant portions of the original article or email will only annoy others, so simply copy the pertinent portions of the message and paste them into your reply. Most email software automatically sets the excerpt with carets (<>).

Always include your *signature* at the bottom of email messages. Your signature should include your name, position, affiliation, and Internet address. Signature files are like customized business cards. You can attach them to newsgroup or mailing list posts and to email messages. Signature files should be no more than four lines long. For professional purposes, a signature should have the same information as a business card: name, title, postal and/or email address, and a telephone or fax number. For personal or fun uses, a signature file could contain a favorite quote or musical lyric, a poem, or even a short piece of ASCII art created with keyboard characters. Keep it short though.

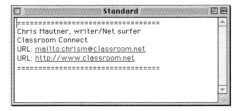

A warning: Be careful using sarcasm and humor. Without face-to-face communication, an email joke may be viewed as criticism.

Another way to express emotion is to capitalize words, but do so only to highlight an important point or to distinguish a title or heading. Some users consider all caps to be SHOUTING. *Asterisks* surrounding a word can also be used to add emphasis and make a stronger point.

Express Yourself

A cardinal rule for communicating on the Internet is *keep it short*. Does that leave tools like email completely devoid of personality, emotion, or humor? Absolutely not. There are several ways to express your feelings over email. Two primary means are your signature file (mentioned above) and *smileys*, also known as *emoticons*. Both can be used in any email communication.

Smileys are normal type characters that, when viewed sideways, resemble facial expressions. Here are some of the more common ones and their meanings. You can come up with dozens more.

:-)	A basic smiley, used to express happiness or sarcasm
;-)	A winking smiley, suggesting an "inside joke"
:-(	A frown
B-)	Wearing glasses

In addition to smileys, numerous abbreviations or acronyms are commonly used on the Internet, including:

CUL	See You Later
FAQ	Frequently Asked Question
FYI	For Your Information
FYA	For Your Amusement
IMHO	In My Humble Opinion
IOW	In Other Words
OTOH	On The Other Hand
TIA	Thanks In Advance

While it's impossible to instantly pick up on all of the acronyms and smileys that are online, it'll only take a little time before you can gain command of this unique Cyberspace pseudo-language!

Mailing Lists

A mailing list is an email-based public or private forum on a particular topic, and there are 600,000 different ones! Each one is like an electronic newspaper or newsletter consisting entirely of reader submissions. Educators can join any of the hundreds of mailing lists having to do with education. (See Chapter 4, Educational Resources, for an exhaustive list.)

Mailing lists are interactive because a subscriber anywhere in the world can read messages posted to it and can send messages to the list. Anyone with an email account can join a mailing list, though some are only open to members of certain organizations.

To join a mailing list, you must email a message to a mailing list's "subscription" email address and request to be added to the subscriber list. After the message is received, you are automatically added to the list.

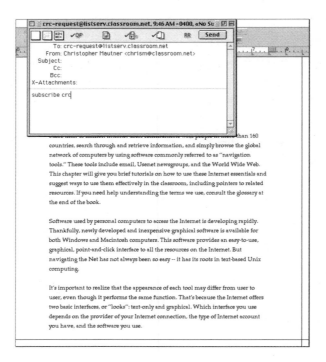

than 160 countries, search through and retrieve information, and simply browse the global network of computers by using software commonly referred to as "navigation tools." These tools include email, Usenet newsgroups, and the World Wide Web. This chapter will give you brief tutorials on how to use these Internet essentials and suggest ways to use them effectively in the classroom, including pointers to related resources. If you need help understanding the terms we use, consult the glossary at the end of the book.

Software used by personal computers to access the Internet is developing rapidly. Thankfully, newly developed and inexpensive graphical software is available for both Windows and Macintosh computers. This software provides an easy-to-use, graphical, point-and-click interface to all the resources on the Internet. But navigating the Net has not always been so easy -- it has its roots in text-based Unix computing.

It's important to realize that the appearance of each tool may differ from user to user, even though it performs the same function. That's because the Internet offers two basic interfaces, or "looks": text-only and graphical. Which interface you use depends on the provider of your Internet connection, the type of Internet account you have, and the software you use.

The first message you will receive will be a confirmation message from the list's owner. Hang onto this message! It contains important information, including instructions on how to send messages to the list and guidelines or rules for subscribers. It also tells you how to temporarily suspend mailings (if you are going away on a trip, for example) and permanently unsubscribe or delete your name from the list.

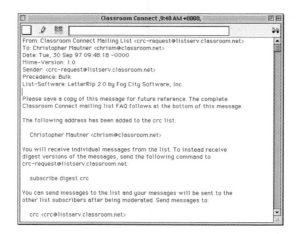

Subscribers participate in discussions by reading messages and posting their responses to the list itself rather than by replying individually to the other subscribers. The list automatically rebroadcasts a copy of any posted message to all subscribers.

Mailing lists can be moderated or unmoderated. On unmoderated lists, messages (also called "posts") are automatically broadcast to every subscriber. On moderated lists, posts are monitored by the list owner, who serves as a gatekeeper. Only messages the moderator believes are appropriate are broadcast to all subscribers on the list. A rejected message is returned with a message explaining why it was refused. This gives the subscriber a chance to change and resend it.

Educators will find mailing lists to be a great resource for professional development and networking. You can ask questions, discuss teaching methods and curriculum development, and launch online classroom projects with others around the world.

Students studying other languages can interact with native-speaking students from other lands. There are dozens of age-appropriate and topic-specific mailing lists offering a wide variety of information. Schools can even start their own mailing lists.

Subscribing to a mailing is simple. For instance, if you wanted to subscribe to the AAAE (American Association for Agricultural Education) list, you could send an email message from your browser to this address.

mailto:listserv@listserv.net

(If you were already in your email window, you would type in the address above, but omit the "mailto:" part of the address.)

Next, you would type **subscribe AAAE John Smith** on the first line of the body of the message. Where you see **John Smith** you would type your name. You will be added to the subscriber list immediately and receive your first messages within hours. All mailing lists have different procedures for subscribing. To find a list of discussion groups for educators, connect to these Web sites:

http://www.liszt.com

http://tile.net/listserv

Spend several days reading the posts to the list until you get a feel for the "personality" of the list. Your first post should be a short introduction of yourself so other subscribers can get to know you. After that, feel free to post regularly, but be sure to stay within the context of the list topic.

Mailing List Netiquette

Some mailing lists have low rates of traffic, while others can flood an email box with several hundred messages per day. The barrage of messages for multiple subscribers of mailing lists at the same school requires extensive system processing and disk space, which can tie up valuable resources.

Allowing all interested teachers to individually subscribe to a list can overwhelm the school's system. It may be better for one teacher or librarian to subscribe and then allow everyone to access the list's posts. When you subscribe, use your personal email account. Don't subscribe using a shared school account unless you know everyone wants to read the list. When signing up for a group, save your subscription confirmation letter for reference. The message cites the rules of the list as well as instructions on how to suspend mail and unsubscribe from the list.

When going away for more than a week, unsubscribe or suspend mail from any mailing lists or listserv services. Occasionally subscribers who are unfamiliar with netiquette will submit requests to subscribe or unsubscribe directly to the list itself. Such requests should be made to the appropriate address, not the list posting address.

Keep the questions and comments that you send to the list relevant to the focus of the discussion group. Resist the temptation to "flame" others on the list. These discussions are public and meant for constructive exchanges. Treat others as you would want them to treat you. When requesting a list of information from subscribers, ask that responses be directed to you personally, offering to post a summary or answer to your question to the group later.

When replying to a message posted to a discussion group, check the address to be certain your reply will go only to the intended location, person, or group. Simply selecting "reply" will usually send your message to the entire subscriber list. Many times it is more appropriate to answer another subscriber's question or to communicate with that subscriber by sending email to him or her directly. This will reduce the extraneous traffic on the list. Twenty people answering the same question on a large list can quickly fill your mailbox and everyone else's too.

About Usenet Newsgroups

Newsgroups, or Usenet newsgroups as they are officially called, follow the same principle as mailing lists, except that users don't receive individual messages in their email boxes. Newsgroups are like giant, world-wide bulletin boards that anyone on the Internet or a commercial online service can read and post to.

An estimated ten million people from around the globe can read and post to any of more than 29,000 newsgroups covering an incredible range of topics. Newsgroups are circulated around the world to tens of thousands of computer sites known as news servers, which are paid for by your Internet Service Provider or commercial online service. Any individual user of those news servers can choose to read any article, as the message postings are called, from any one of the newsgroup topics, and then post a reply. That reply is then circulated to every other news server in the world.

It's important to note that not every site receives all postings and that some newsgroups are regional, circulating only throughout a particular geographic area.

It's easy to find the newsgroups you need because they are arranged in alphabetical order by words that describe their topics. For example, the newsgroup **comp.systems.amiga** is dedicated to Amiga computer systems, while **comp.systems.mac** refers to Apple Macintosh computers.

Here's what the K12.chat.teacher newsgroup looks like through Netscape.

A newsgroup exists for just about any topic imaginable, from literature to pop culture to education. Due to the subject matter of some groups, many are *not* appropriate for K-12 users, so supervision is critical. As with mailing lists, most newsgroups post a general information document highlighting what's accepted and what's not. In some groups anything is acceptable, while others have stringent requirements. The rules are usually outlined in the group's Frequently Asked Questions (FAQ) document.

Newsgroups are where the majority of Net flaming — the sending of nasty, hateful messages — occurs. Thus, it's best to monitor a newsgroup or "lurk" for a while to get a feel for its atmosphere and what sort of conduct is accepted. (See Chapter 4 for a comprehensive list of newsgroups for K-12 educators.)

Newsgroup Classifications

alt. Alt. groups are generally defined as alternatives to the mainstream groups listed below. They're easier to create, so the door is open to all sorts of off-the-wall, strange, or down right chaotic discussions.

comp. These newsgroups are primarily about computers and are frequented by computer professionals and hobbyists.

k12. Here you'll find discussions related to K-12 students and educators and the subjects they teach and learn about.

sci. Discussions in the sci. groups focus on the sciences, ranging from biology to nuclear physics.

misc. Newsgroups classified as misc. are usually ones that don't fit into any other category.

soc. These newsgroups deal with social science issues.

talk. The talk. newsgroups usually feature lots of continuing debates or flame wars on a variety of topics.

news. These newsgroups have to do with the Usenet news network itself.

rec. Stands for recreational. An example is **rec.hobby.sewing.**

Telnet and MOOs

Back in the days before the World Wide Web, telnet was a popular tool that allowed users to connect to a computer in the next room or halfway around the world and use it as if they were sitting at its keyboard. While no longer the Internet darling it once was, telnet is still a useful tool, if only because it allows you to take advantage of one of the more interesting online educational terrains — MOOs.

A MOO is a virtual, text-based environment where users around the world can connect to a computer simultaneously and interact with each other by typing commands and messages. MOOs emphasize social interaction and the ability of users to create their own virtual objects, allowing students to create and explore their own "virtual communities."

In some ways, MOOs resemble that other interactive Internet tool — Internet Relay Chat (IRC). They allow users to communicate with each other over the computer in real time. For educators though, MOOs are often a better option than IRC. They are not as technically challenging, are easier to monitor, and offer a much more controlled atmosphere than a free-wheeling chat room on an IRC server. Students experience the excitement of alive online chat but in a controlled, structured, educational setting.

In order to use telnet via Netscape, you'll need to have a separate telnet program installed on your computer. A variety of such programs is available, and several of them, like MacMoose, are designed specifically for use in a MOO environment. Be sure to ask your Internet provider for the address of their nearest site containing telnet software for your computer.

MacMoose

http://www.cc.gatech.edu/fac/Amy.Bruckman/moose-crossing/

Nifty Telnet

http://andrew2.andrew.cmu.edu/dist/niftytelnet.html

If you come across a telnet address while surfing the Web, enter it into your browser in this fashion.

telnet://logos.daedalus.com:7777

By putting **telnet://** in front of the telnet address, Netscape recognizes it as a telnet site address and will open up your telnet software ASAP.

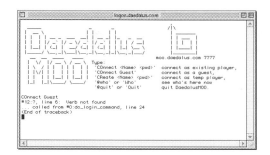

You'll probably start your Internet travels with a list of sites to visit, so you'll already know the required passwords. As you build your own roster of favorite telnet and MOO sites, make sure to note the login and password requirements. For many sites, logging in as **Guest** and using **Guest** as the password will work.

It's also helpful to jot down the commands used for navigating a particular site. MOO menus are text-based, so you must enter keys or numbers to get around — for example, **PgDn** to scroll down the screen, or **Q** or **X** to quit or exit. These commands are usually shown at the bottom of each screen, or you can type **Help** or **?** to get a list.

In addition to these commands, there are some other commands that are specific to MOOs. You can get a list of these directions by sending an email message to the Classroom Connect infobot. (Remember to delete the "mailto:" portion of the address if you are already in your email window.)

mailto:info@classroom.com

Type **send moocommands** in the body of the message.

Once you and your students have become accustomed to the world of MOOs, the educational possibilities are great. You can collaborate with other teachers and administrators in real time about various projects and labs; explore virtual rooms where students can tour famous cities, participate in lab experiments, meet fictional characters, or create your own buildings, games, robots, even whole worlds. MOOs contain a built-in programming language that allows visitors to create their own objects and places.

Be sure that your students have plenty of time to practice and get accustomed to any MOO they may visit. Make sure they are aware of the basic MOO netiquette, have copies of the basic commands, and know what to do if they need help or need to respond to someone bothering them. By starting with a few simple tours and commands, students will be able to build a strong knowledge of the virtual community. For more information about Moos, connect to these Web sites.

http://www.daedalus.com/net/MOOTIPS.html

http://lucien.sims.berkeley.edu/moo.html

The Future of the Internet: Video and Audio Conferencing

Remember those science fiction movies of yore where people talked to each other over a video screen or computer instead of the telephone? Thanks to the Internet, that fiction is now fast becoming a reality. Inexpensive computer conferencing hardware and software has been appearing on store shelves all over the world, making this exciting technology available for educators to use in their classrooms for the first time. By attaching a small video camera and microphone to your computer, you and your students can talk with other schools thousands of miles away, all for the cost of a local phone call!

In the past, chatting with other computer users in real time meant that savvy "Internauts" had to rely on Internet Relay Chat (IRC) — a complicated online system that allowed users to type messages to each other back and forth across their computer screens. New types of software, however, remove the need to use IRC. Why type messages to someone when you can view and listen with them via your computer just as easily?

Using audio and video conferencing software, Internet users can:

- Consult or interview experts in a particular field (such as anthropology) in real time
- Connect your students with their peers in the next state or anywhere around the world
- Share skits, projects, and discussions with several different classrooms at once
- Watch and listen to live press conferences, newscasts, and concerts
- Hold professional meetings with people from anywhere in the world!

Right now several different types of conference software are available. Some only allow for audio hookup. Others provide for audio and video conferencing. Some are expensive, but many more are offered free to educators or at least have a free demo version that can be downloaded over the Internet.

Audio Conferencing Software

Audio conferencing software allows Net users to turn their computers into a telephone. Using this technology, you can call people from across the globe without having to pay high priced long distance phone bills. All you need is a computer outfitted with a sound card, microphone, modem, and an Internet connection.

In general, audio conferencing programs work by digitizing your speech as you talk and sending the signals over the Internet. For an overview of all audio conferencing software now available on the Net, check out the Web sites below.

Audio Conference Sites

The Virtual Voice

http://www.virtual-voice.com

The Internet Telephony Consortium

http://itel.mit.edu

How Can I Use the Internet as a Telephone?

http://rpcp.mit.edu/~asears/voice-faq.html

Video Conferencing Software

The prices for most Internet video software products are amazingly high — from $550 to $4,000. There is, however, one product that's in use in thousands of schools to accomplish the same task — CU-SeeMe. With this free software and an inexpensive video camera, you can see and talk in real time with another CU-SeeMe site from any corner of the globe.

Download CU-SeeMe

ftp://gated.cornell.edu/pub/video/

To operate CU-SeeMe, you will need a video input device and a microphone. You can run the software without either of these things, but you won't be able to converse with anyone, and they won't be able to see you, though you will be able to "lurk" and watch and listen in. The Connectix QuickCam, which retails for $99, is the best video camera and microphone combination currently available.

CU-SeeMe Headquarters

http://cu-seeme.cornell.edu

Connectix QuickCam

http://www.connectix.com

It is possible to confer with several other users at the same time, just as you would enter an IRC chat room to chat with different groups of people. To take part in a group conference, you need to visit one of the many reflector sites on the Internet, which are dedicated servers that monitor and process the various videoconferencing connections simultaneously. Once you've logged on, you can send pictures, audio, and text to the reflector, which then transmits the information to the other participants.

Cornell University Reflector

132.236.91.204

NASA TV Select Online Reflector #1

1139.88.27.43

NASA TV Select Online Reflector #2

158.36.33.5

ABC World News Now

192.215.2.250

When connecting to a reflector site or individual, don't be surprised if there is no response or the site is full. Reflectors can only accommodate up to eight active participants, so you might be out of luck unless you've made a previous arrangement with a school or reflector site.

Although you can download and use the latest beta version of CU-SeeMe via the Cornell ftp site, an enhanced commercial version of CU-SeeMe is also available. This "for-pay" version, which includes color video, costs about $99. In addition, it also allows users to exchange text documents, spreadsheets, and pictures with online participants using built-in "whiteboarding" software. You can even add your own comments and changes to these documents — as if you all were in the same room! A demo version of CU-SeeMe for Windows and Mac is available at the White Pine Web site.

White Pine

http://www.wpine.com

Unfortunately, neither audio nor video software will work very well if you have a computer with a small amount of memory or a slow bandwidth speed. You need at least a 28.8 modem to be able to use this software properly, and even then it can seem rather slow and halting at times. Ideally, you should have an ISDN, 56k, or T1 line to audio and video conference effectively.

Video Conferencing Web Sites

Both the free and for-pay versions of CU-SeeMe come with a list of current reflector site addresses, but the sites below will prove useful for finding some video friends as well.

CU-SeeMe Audio-Video Conferencing

http://www.indstate.edu/msattler/sci-tech/comp/CU-SeeMe

CU-SeeMe Reflector List

http://storm.cis.fordham.edu/reflector.list.html

CU-SeeMe Schools

http://www.gsn.org/gsn/cu/index.html

Elements of an Effective CU-SeeMe Conference

http://www.gsn.org/teach/articles/videoconf.html

Items for Cu-SeeMe Users

http://www.jungle.com/msattler/eshop/catalog-pages/cuseeme-items.html

World Wide Web Tours

A WALK THROUGH FIVE RICH INTERNET SITES FOR EDUCATORS

Nothing beats actually visiting a place you've read or heard about. After all, while you may have seen plenty of commercials about Jamaica, you haven't experienced the island until you've strolled its lily-white beaches or caught a wave off the coast.

The same holds true for Internet sites. Several books have been published listing great educational sites and their Internet addresses, but they don't actually take you inside to explore them, understand how teachers can use the information, and learn how to get around. These virtual tours do just that.

In this chapter of the *Educator's Internet Companion*, we will take you on a guided tour of some of the biggest and best educational sites on the Internet. At the same time, we'll show you how to ride the World Wide Web via your Internet browser (Netscape Navigator or Microsoft Internet Explorer).

TOUR I: *The White House*

The White House Web site is the official online guide to the inner workings of the U.S. Presidency. It features an interactive tour of the building, biographical information about past presidents, and information about the executive branch's latest initiatives.

Internet navigation tool: World Wide Web

Site Address: http://www.whitehouse.gov

Sign on to the Internet and load your Netscape or Internet Explorer software. In the location window, type **http://www.whitehouse.gov** as your destination and hit return.

Welcome to the home page of the U.S. Presidency! Notice that the Title Bar tells you where you are — at the "Welcome to the White House" page. To start our tour, click on the **President and Vice-President** hyperlink.

From here we can visit the offices of the President, Vice-President, the First Lady, and Mrs. Gore. Let's click on the icon of Bill Clinton to see what's inside the **Executive Office of the President.**

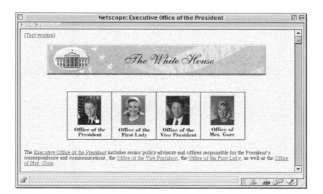

There's some pretty interesting information here that could be easily incorporated into any social studies class, including information on Clinton's accomplishments and initiatives and transcripts of his public addresses. Head back to the previous page by clicking on the **Back** button.

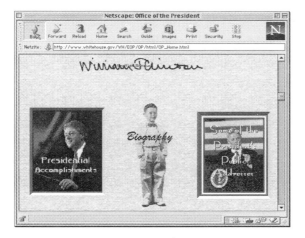

Here we are back at the Office of the President page. Notice that the link to Bill Clinton's page has turned from blue to purple. The change in color tells us that we've already followed that link.

At the bottom of the page, there's information on sending electronic mail to the president. Click on **The President** link to continue.

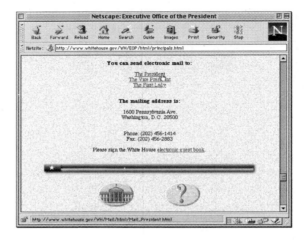

Now here's a truly interactive site! By filling out this form and hitting the send button at the bottom of the page, we can send a message to the president of the United States.

After reading this page over, head back to the White House home page. To do that, go up to the Go menu, and select **Welcome to the White House.**

Here we are back at the home page! Click on the **White House for Kids** link at the bottom of the page to continue. When the next page downloads, click on the White House for Kids icon (featuring a cartoon version of Socks the cat).

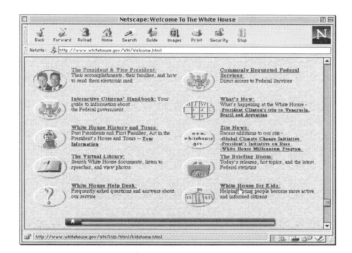

Here's a kid-sized version of the White House Web site, complete with a history of the building, information on the president, and pets that have resided in the White House. This seems like a perfect Web site for elementary students learning about the U.S. government!

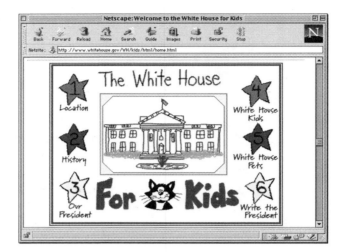

Be sure to explore all the offerings here before moving on to the next tour. If you decide you'd like to come back to this Web site, save the address by bookmarking the site. To do that, simply select **Add Bookmark** from the bookmark menu.

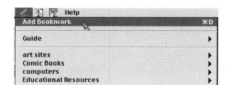

TOUR II: Department of Education

The U.S. Department of Education's home site on the World Wide Web has links to some of the most important educational developments and programs in the country, as well as a variety of online services and guides.

Internet navigation tool: World Wide Web

Site address: http://www.ed.gov

Sign on to the Internet and load your Netscape or Internet Explorer software. In the location window, type **http://www.ed.gov** as your destination, and hit return.

This site is a real find, with more than 20 separate links to education information, from a list of National Education Goals to selected congressional testimony and speeches for the Secretary of Education.

At the left side of the screen, press the News & Events button.

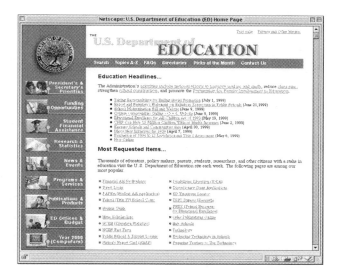

Here's the latest news from the Department of Education! Feel free to peruse this site, then, to continue the tour, head back to the home page by clicking the **Back** button twice or by typing **www.ed.gov** in the location window of your browser.

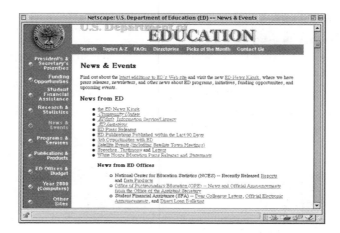

Let's browse this year's **Student Financial Assistance.** Click on those words on the left side navigation bar of the homepage..

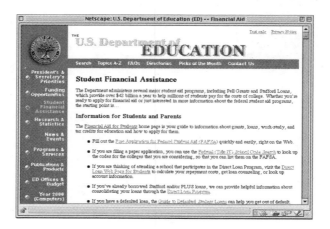

Scroll down to the item called **Direct Loans,** and click on it to continue.

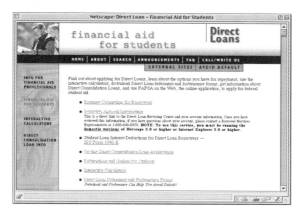

Here's complete information about Direct Loans available from the federal government. Read through to get a feel for what's here. Click on **Interactive Calculators** and explore the online budget calculators available to your students..

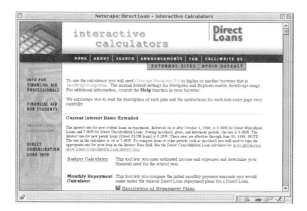

Did you know that the Department of Education maintains a text-based site in addition to this one? These type of sites are called **gopher** sites, as people visit them to "go for" information. To get there, enter **gopher://gopher.ed.gov** into the location window of your browser. (Note that we just tacked **gopher://** on the front of the address instead of http://.)

The Department's gopher menu appears. Click on **Educational Software** to continue.

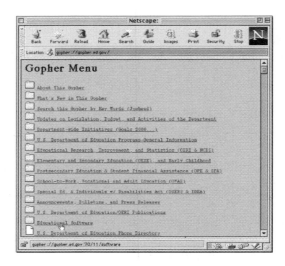

Here's a huge collection of free educational software for five popular computer platforms, including IBM PCs running Windows and Macintosh computers. Enjoy!

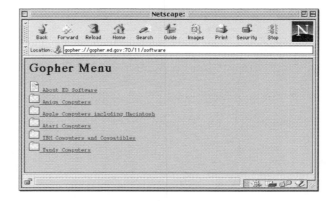

How to access the Department of Education

http://www.ed.gov

gopher://gopher.ed.gov

Tour III: ERIC

The AskERIC Virtual Library gives visitors graphical access to everything the Educational Resource and Information Center (ERIC) offers.

Internet Navigation Tool: World Wide Web

Site address: http://ericir.syr.edu

Sign on to the Internet and load your Netscape or Internet Explorer software. Then, in the location window, type **http://ericir.syr.edu** as your destination, and hit return.

You've arrived at the AskERIC home page. Click once on the **AskERIC Virtual Library** icon to begin your tour.

The entire site is broken down into several different sections for easy Web surfing. Take a look at each item, then select **AskERIC InfoGuides** at the top of the page. After that page downloads, select the **"complete archive of AskERIC InfoGuides."**

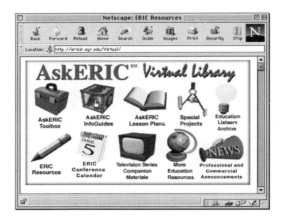

Here are hundreds of individual indexes to information ranging from African History to Full Day Kindergarten to Vocational Education and Whole Language. As you scroll through the list, note the functional toolbar at the bottom of the document. You can use it to quickly move to each of the site's main areas. Click on **Astronomy for Secondary** located in the list of InfoGuides.

Here's an excellent document you can use to track down Astronomy resources on the Internet for use in a secondary school environment. Print a copy for yourself or a colleague! Be sure to check out any other InfoGuides that are of interest to you as well.

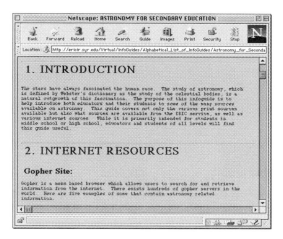

Click on the little left arrow button at the top of your screen a few times to step backwards until you return to the main menu or home page. Then click on the **About AskERIC** icon. From there, scroll down the page until you see the link for the **AskERIC Slide Show.** Click on that link to let the site take you on a tour.

Now, click on the **Slideshow's General Overview** icon to begin the tour.

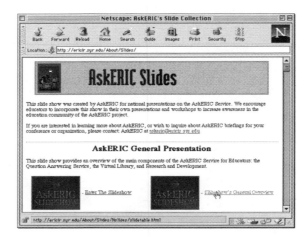

After you read each slide, click on the word **Next** to move forward. Enjoy the tour!

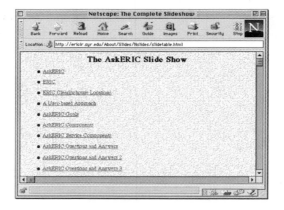

Phone: (800) 464-9107, (315) 443-3640

mailto:askeric@ericir.syr.edu

http://ericir.syr.edu

TOUR IV: Diversity University

Diversity University is an educational MOO that allows students and teachers to communicate and travel through a text-based environment.

Internet navigation tool: Telnet

Site address: telnet://moo.du.org:8888

Navigation software used: Standard, text-based telnet software

Sign on to the Internet and load your Netscape or Internet Explorer software. Then, in the location window, type **http://moo.du.org** as your destination, and hit return. Once that Web page loads up, click on the **Visiting Diversity University** link, located near the bottom of the page.

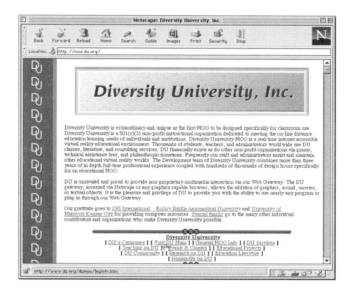

From here, click on the **Visit DU (by telnet) now** link with your mouse. If you have your telnet software properly installed, it should load up and take you straight to the front page of the DU MOO.

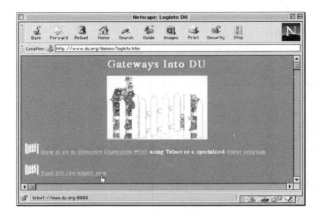

After logging into the University, you will be presented with the following message. Type **co guest** and then hit return.

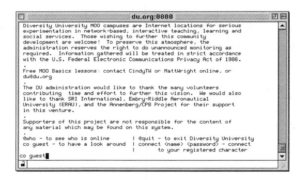

You will then be presented with the main menu, which includes a short list of dos and don'ts while you're exploring this particular MOO. Hit return to agree to the conditions and continue.

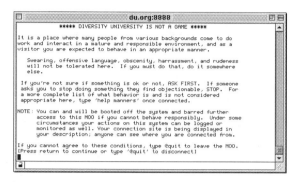

Now you have officially entered the MOO. A brief paragraph tells you that you are currently in Quiet Cubicle No. 3. Note that it also shows you the different directions you can travel in (**"out"**), and lists what's in the room. Currently there is a note in the room with you. To read the note, type **read note** and hit return.

This helpful little note explains how to operate some of the virtual objects you'll encounter on you're travels through the University. Now it's time to head out of the room and into the Orientation Center. To do that, type **out** and hit return.

Now we are in the Orientation Center. It appears that another person, **Jacinth_Guest,** is here with us. To say hello to him, we'll type **to Jacinth_Guest hello.**

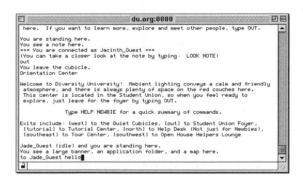

Isn't that nice — Jacinth_Guest saw our message and typed hello back. Before we get too involved in an online conversation, however, we should probably become a little familiar with the area. To get a list of instructions, type **help newbie.**

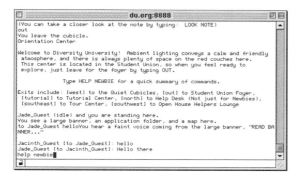

```
du.org:8888
(You can take a closer look at the note by typing:  LOOK NOTE)
out
You leave the cubicle.
Orientation Center

Welcome to Diversity University!  Ambient lighting conveys a calm and friendly
  atmosphere, and there is always plenty of space on the red couches here.
  This center is located in the Student Union, so when you feel ready to
  explore, just leave for the foyer by typing OUT.

          Type HELP NEWBIE for a quick summary of commands.

Exits include: [west] to the Quiet Cubicles, [out] to Student Union Foyer,
  [tutorial] to Tutorial Center, [north] to Help Desk (Not just for Newbies),
  [southeast] to Tour Center, [southwest] to Open House Helpers Lounge

Jade_Guest (idle) and you are standing here.
You see a large banner, an application folder, and a map here.
to Jade_Guest helloYou hear a faint voice coming from the large banner, "READ BA
NNER..."

Jacinth_Guest [to Jade_Guest]: hello
Jade_Guest [to Jacinth_Guest]: Hello there
help newbie
```

Here's a helpful list of commands we can use to move around Diversity University and interact with the other people visiting here. When we first entered this room, it mentioned a banner hanging on the wall. To read the banner, simply type **read banner** and hit return.

```
du.org:8888
Moving    Type one of the directions in the [ ] of the exits
          listing shown when you enter: look
@who      To see who else is currently in the MOO and where they are,
          type @WHO
@quit     To disconnect from the MOO, simply type @QUIT
Paging    If you wish to talk to someone who is not in the same
          room, you can use  PAGE <PERSON> <MESSAGE>
          EX: page Jeanne Hi, how are you?
@info     Get some information about a person, with  @INFO <PERSON>
Mailing   You can also send a MOOmail message to someone by typing
          @SEND <PERSON>  You will be prompted for a subject line
          for your message and then put into the Mail Room.  When in
          the Mail Room, write your message as if you were speaking
          to someone (put SAY in front of each line).  When you're
          done, to send your message, type SEND
Helpme    Our "helpful people system" will send your message to
          people who can help you.  For help with basic MOO usage,
          try: helpme basic
Help      Help is available on a wide range of topics.   HELP INDEX
          will provide a list all available help listings.
Garbled?  If you are having trouble with text from the MOO messing
          up what you are trying to type. Type  HELP OUTPUT to see
          how to control that.
read banner
```

Here we're presented with a list of commands we can use to learn about this virtual environment. If we want the full tour, we can type tutorial. This time, however, let's type **help poi.**

Typing that command brought up information about the Points of Interest (POI) board, a helpful object used to locate interesting locations within Diversity University. Let's get an idea of what locations they offer by typing **poi-look.** When the list of categories comes up, choose **1** to get the full index.

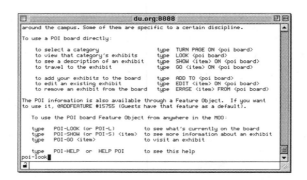

Wow! They sure have a lot of interesting rooms here at DU! I think I noticed one of the rooms was based on T. S. Eliot's poem, *The Wasteland*. That sounds interesting. To get to that room, we simply type **poi-go 68** (the official number of the Wasteland room).

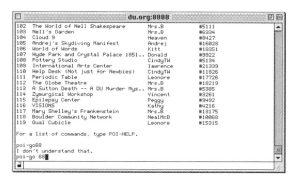

```
                          du.org:8888
102   The World of Nell Shakespeare      Mrs.B      #5111
103   Nell's Garden                      Mrs.B      #6334
104   Cloud 9                            Heaven     #8427
105   Andrej's Skydiving Manifest        Andrej     #16028
106   World of Words                     Kitt       #18351
107   Hyde Park and Crystal Palace 1851..Donald     #9822
108   Pottery Studio                     CindyTW    #5134
109   International Arts Center           lawrence   #21339
110   Help Desk (Not just for Newbies)   CindyTW    #11826
111   Periodic Table                     Leonore    #17726
112   The Globe Theatre                  Mrs.B      #18219
113   A Sutton Death -- A DU Murder Mys..Mrs.B      #5385
114   Zymurgical Workshop                Vincent    #3261
115   Epilepsy Center                    Peggy      #9492
116   VISIONS                            Kathy      #4216
117   Mary Shelley's Frankenstein        Mrs.B      #13175
118   Boulder Community Network          NealMcB    #10068
119   Qual Cubicle                       Leonore    #15315

For a list of commands, type POI-HELP.

poi-go68
I don't understand that.
poi-go 68█
```

Here we are, inside a virtual landscape based on Eliot's poem! From here we can tour the area, talk to the fortune teller, or head off into one of the adjoining rooms. If at any point we want to head back to our original starting point, we just type **home.** Any time we want to leave the University, we simply type **@quit.**

```
                          du.org:8888
[It is April in T.S. Eliot's THE WASTE LAND].]
April is the #cruellest month, breeding
Lilacs out of the dead land, mixing
Memory and desire, stirring
Dull roots with spring rain.
[You probably prefer #winter--or even #summer.]

The Waste Land
[You are trapped in a desert waste land, though there are distant #mountains.]
What are the roots that clutch, what branches grow
Out of this stony rubbish?  Son [/daughter] of man,
You cannot say, or guess, for you know only
A heap of broken #images . . .
[It's very hot.  Perhaps you should take shelter under that big #rock.]
   [NOTE:  by convention, items marked with an asterick are "details"
       that can be looked at by typing, for example, 'look images' or
       'l images'--You can also 'look' at exits and objects "seen" in the
       area, like the tent here.  Comments to owner--see @info RobtC]
Exits include: [out] to Special Collections Room, [north] to Unreal City,
[west] to Las Vegas, [cube] to Moo Poetry Cube
RobtC (sleeping) is standing here.
You see a fortune-teller's tent and sign (type 'look sign') here.
You have arrived at ????.
█
```

mailto:dusvcs@du.org
http://www.du.org
telnet://moo.du.org:8888

TOUR V: Shareware.com

Shareware.com is an interactive Web site, sponsored by C/Net, that offers visitors the ability to search through and download software from its index of almost 200,000 different titles.

Internet navigation tool: World Wide Web

Site Address: http://shareware.com

Sign on to the Internet and load your Netscape or Internet Explorer software. In the location window, type **http://shareware.com** as your destination, and hit return.

Here we are at the site's front entrance. For this particular tour, we will be looking for educational software, so in the search box at the top of the page, type the word **education,** select what type of computer you're using (in this case Macintosh), and hit return.

Here's an impressive sampling of the variety of software that is available for the K-12 educator! The second software offering is **Ten Thumbs Typing Tutor 2.1;** let's click on that link.

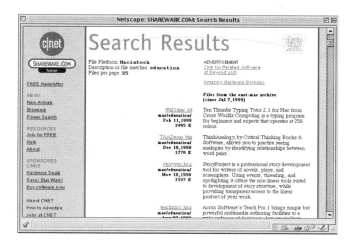

Clicking on that hyperlink took us to this page, which provides us with information about where the software is located, and how reliable they are. Click on the link to download the software demonstration.

Notice that his file has the extension **.sea.hqx.** This extension means that the file has been compressed in some fashion. In the Windows world, .zip is the most common compression method.

In order to use any of these files, you will need to expand them to your hard drive. For Mac, a program known as Stuffit Expander does the trick and usually comes free of charge when you download or purchase your Internet browser. Windows users should get a program called UnZip, which should come with their copy of Netscape or Internet Explorer.

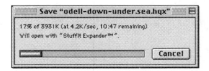

After waiting about five minutes or so, the file is downloaded onto your computer desktop and automatically uncompressed by Stuffit Expander. From here, all you have to do is double click on the software's icon, and you're up and running!

If your file doesn't automatically expand, don't worry. Just drag the unstuffed icon over to your Stuffit Expander icon. You can keep your new document on your desktop or put it into a folder with the rest of your Internet applications.

Be sure to examine some of the other educational shareware available at Shareware.com. If you do decide to keep the software, always remember to pay the shareware fee!

Access to Shareware.com

http://shareware.com

We hope you've enjoyed the tours. These sites give only a hint of the valuable resources the Internet offers K–12 educators. Now that you know more about navigating the Net, go to Chapter 4, Educational Resources, pick out some sites that interest you, and take a few self-guided tours!

AN EXTENSIVE LIST OF INTERNET SITES, MAILING LISTS, AND NEWSGROUPS FOR EDUCATORS

The number of resources on the Internet is exploding. According to one estimate, more than 40,000 new Internet services and information locations come online every month. Hundreds of them are related to education.

Many Internet sites are valuable to educators — even those that don't seem so at first glance. The staff of Classroom Connect constantly searches for sites with lesson plans, text documents, software, and other sources that will enrich the classroom experience for students.

This chapter is a compilation of resources found after more than 1,000 hours of Net surfing. It includes the addresses and brief descriptions of extensive mailing lists and newsgroups covering topics of interest to educators and students.

Remember, the Internet is an evolving community. Addresses and list names, up-to-date when printed, are subject to change at any time. Patience and persistence count when you're on the Internet!

Educational MOOs

A MOO is a text-based, virtual environment where users can communicate and move about by typing commands back and forth in real time. Because MOOs focus on social interaction and conferencing, many educators use them as a virtual classroom setting — especially if their students are located several miles away. Below are just a few of the educational MOOs available. To access a MOO, you'll need telnet software, which can be easily obtained from the download.com Web site.

http://download.com

BayMOO

telnet://baymoo.sfsu.edu:8888
Operating from the San Francisco Bay area, BayMOO is a humanities MOO whose purposes include: building a virtual community based on respect; constructing interesting virtual objects; hosting conferences and classes; and promoting the exchange of ideas on a wide range of social, artistic, and technical subjects.

BioMOO

telnet://bioinfo.weizmann.ac.il:8888/

A virtual academy for biologists. BioMoo is a place to meet colleagues in biology studies and related fields and brainstorm, hold colloquia and conferences, and explore the serious side of this new medium.

Connections MOO

telnet://connections.sensemedia.net:3333
http://www.ucet.ufl.edu/~tari/connections/connections-home.html

Connections seeks to provide an alternative learning environment for classrooms as well as special interest groups and projects whose subject matter falls outside the boundaries of school. Any class of any level studying any subject is welcome here. Students can use the MOO to meet as a full class or in small groups, work on projects, meet with others, and so on.

Diversity University

telnet://moo.du.org:8888
http://moo.du.org

This online university is specifically designed to provide an online environment where teachers and their students can work. Visitors can take a tour of the human brain, perform science experiments, travel through Dante's Inferno and T. S. Eliot's Wasteland, or just hang out in the student lounge and chat with other teachers. An excellent MOO for those who are inexperienced with the technology.

LinguaMOO

telnet://lingua.utdallas.edu:8888
http://lingua.utdallas.edu

LinguaMOO is an educational and professional community for teachers and students in the Rhetoric and Writing program at The University of Texas in Dallas. It is both a learning environment and a place where faculty collaborate on various projects related to teaching and research using electronic media.

MediaMOO

telnet://purple-crayon.media.mit.edu:8888

MediaMOO provides a place for those who are interested in integrating technology, education, and writing. Every Tuesday, users gather informally in the Netoric cafe to talk about these issues and other writing-related topics. This site is more appropriate for teachers and researchers than students.

MiamiMOO

telnet://moo.cas.muohio.edu:7777
http://miamimoo.mcs.muohio.edu

Feel like exploring ancient Greece or Asia? MiamiMOO allows students and instructors to reconstruct historical sites and reenact the events that transpired there. You can also visit 18th century England or ancient India.

MicroMUSE: A Virtual Reality Adventure Game

telnet://michael.ai.mit.edu

A combination of a real-time "chat" group and a role-playing science fiction game. The user enters the twenty-fourth century world of MicroMUSE and meets characters who inhabit the space colony. MicroMUSE may acquaint a student with computer networking as well as provide an exercise in creativity because students communicate, explore, and design their own corner of this cyberspace microworld.

MOOville

telnet://moo.ucet.ufl.edu:7777
http://www.ucet.ufl.edu/writing/MOO/

Hosted by the University of Florida, MOOville offers a variety of interactive text projects ranging from presentations on Susan B. Anthony and woman's suffrage to race relations. Automated "robots" guide you through these exhibits. MOOville also provides some teachers with their own teaching spaces.

PMC MOO

telnet://hero.village.virginia.edu:7777

This virtual environment is designed to promote multiple explorations of contemporary postmodern theory and practice. Here you can take a dip in the ocean, visit an abandoned UFO, or get on your soapbox at the coffee shop.

schMOOze University

telnet://schmooze.hunter.cuny.edu:8888/

Designed for ESL/EFL students, schMOOze University is a friendly MOO known for its hospitality. Students have opportunities for one-on-one and group conversations as well as access to language games and an on-line dictionary.

Virtual Online University

telnet://athena.edu:8888
http://www.athena.edu

VOU is a nonprofit corporation that engages in two educational missions: Athena University for Higher Education and Athena Preparatory Academy for pre-university education. VOU also functions as a consultant to educational institutions seeking an effective distance learning tool. Check their official Web site for more information on what's available within the virtual campus.

WriteWell

telnet://logos.daedalus.com:7777

http://daedalus.com/index.html

Formerly known as DaedalusMOO, WriteWell is a virtual community where writers meet to have real-time, networked discussions. It is a place where teachers can bring classes who work collaboratively on writing projects, where tutors can meet with writers in interactive, online conferences, and where teachers and rhetoricians can meet with one another to discuss writing in electronic spaces. Teachers planning to bring their classes to DaedalusMOO can create their own teaching space and teaching support materials.

For more information on MOOs, stop by these Web sites:

MOO Tip Sheet for Teachers

http://www.daedalus.com/net/MOOTIPS.html

MOO Central

http://www.pitt.edu/~jrgst7/MOOcentral.html

Educational MOOs/MUDs

http://www.daedalus.com/net/moolist.html

Gurk's MOOGate

http://www4.ncsu.edu/unity/users/a/asdamick/www/moo.html

The Lost Library of MOO

http://lucien.sims.berkeley.edu/moo.html

Yahoo's list of Educational MOOs

http://www.yahoo.com/Education/Instructional_Technology/
Online_Teaching_and_Learning/Educational_MOOs/

Mailing Lists

Internet mailing lists are interactive, email-based discussion groups addressing specific topics. They are interactive because a subscriber anywhere in the world can read messages posted to them and can send a message to the list — all by Internet email.

Anyone with access to Internet email can subscribe to and participate in an Internet mailing list. Users of commercial online services can subscribe. You can search for mailing lists by keyword.

mailto:listserv@cunyvm.cuny.edu

(If you are already in your email window, remember to delete the "mailto:" from these types of addresses.) In the body, type **list global /<keyword>** and leave the subject line blank.

The search will return to you a list of the active mailing lists that match your keyword. Below are just a few of the most popular and heavily used mailing lists for K-12 education.

ASCD Education Bulletin

The Association for Supervision and Curriculum Development currently produces a free, biweekly online newsletter that features brief items of interest to those involved with and who care about K-12 education. Topics covered include curriculum, instruction, assessment, technology, equity, diversity, and continuing support for public schools.

  mailto:majordomo@odie.ascd.org

Type **subscribe bulletin** in the body of the message.

Children Accessing Controversial Information

Can children be prevented from accessing online materials that are controversial? Is preventing access desirable? This list seeks to discuss and resolve these issues. In a short time hundreds of people have joined the list and contributed their thoughts. Hands-on suggestions for implementing filters and supervision methods are the main focus.

  mailto:caci-request@media.mit.edu

Type **subscribe** in the body of the message.

Classroom Connect Mailing List

More than 3,000 online educators have made our free online discussion group a vibrant forum for sharing information about using the Internet in the K-12 classroom. Topics include upcoming projects, safety issues, keypals, and integrating the Net into the curriculum.

  mailto:crc-request@listserv.classroom.com

Type **subscribe digest crc** in the body of the message.

EduPage

A biweekly summary of recent news items on the educational use of computer technology. A very informative, useful resource.

  mailto:listproc@educom.edu

Type **subscribe EDUPAGE <Your Name>** in the body of the message.

Field Trips

This mailing list links K–12 classes to hundreds of other students in the U.S. and abroad. Each class posts detailed messages about its recent field trips and shares its experiences with an interested audience of the same age or grade level. Access to a broad audience of peers motivates students to observe and learn during their trips.

  mailto:majordomo@acme.fred.org

Type **subscribe fieldtrips–L** in the body of the message.

For Your Information: K-12 Education Ideas Using Technology

The Internet may seem like a wonderful tool, but without proper integration in the classroom, it will have little educational value. Enter FYI, a mailing list whose objective is to provide a weekly forum where K-12 educators can share ideas on using technology in the classroom. Each week the digest presents classroom technology integration questions and ideas, Web sites that might be useful to schools, blurbs on other mailing lists of interest, and the latest technology news and trends.

mailto:listserv@ocmvm.cnyric.org

Type **subscribe fyi <Your Name>** in the body of the message.

INCLASS

Sponsored by Canada's SchoolNet Project, INCLASS is a moderated mailing list offering information about using the Internet in the classroom from a Canadian perspective.

mailto:listproc@schoolnet.carleton.ca

Type **subscribe INCLASS <Your Name>** in the body of the message.

International Email Classroom Connections (IECC)

The IECC list is a virtual meeting place for teachers seeking partner classes for international and cross-cultural electronic mail exchanges. This list is different because subscribers and contributors are looking for an entire class of email partners rather than individuals.

mailto:iecc-request@stolaf.edu

Type **subscribe iecc <Your Name>** in the body of the message.

K-12 Student Assessment

This mailing list is an unmoderated online forum for school personnel, researchers, and others interested in issues pertaining to the assessment of student achievement in elementary and secondary schools around the world. The list provides links to online assessment resources, hands-on implementation tips for new assessment measures, and peer support.

mailto:mailserv@lists.cua.edu

Type **subscribe k12assess-L <Your Name>** in the body of your message.

Middle-L

Middle school educators will find the Middle-L online mailing list an indispensable resource. Teachers, administrators, researchers, parents, and others interested in middle school education share ideas, projects, resources, problems, and solutions.

mailto:listserv@listserv.net

Type **subscribe middle-L <Your Name>** in the body of the message.

TeachTech

TeachTech is your one-stop source of computer help from your veteran, computer-savvy peers! If you're having a technical problem with your Macintosh or Windows PC — hardware or software — fire it off to the members of this list. You'll receive an answer to your question within hours, or minutes!

mailto:maiser@coe.memphis.edu

Type **subscribe TeachTech** in the body of your message.

World Wide Web in Education

More than 1,000 educators around the world use this list to discuss how to use the World Wide Web in the K–12 classroom. Recent topics include setting up Web pages at your school, creating Web sites, and more.

mailto:listserv@k12.cnidr.org

Type **subscribe wwwedu <Your Name>** in the body of the message.

Web66 Mailing List

For several years now, the Web66 site has been considered a one-stop online source for all the software and information needed to set up a World Wide Web server at a school. Their new mailing list just underscores this fact by providing K–12 educators and technology coordinators with the opportunity to discuss Web use in their classrooms. Although primarily focused on schools that are implementing and supporting their own Web sites, the list is open to anyone who wants to share Internet questions, ideas, solutions, and projects.

mailto:listserv@tc.umn.edu

Type **sub web66 <Your Name>** in the body of the message.

How to Subscribe to a List

To join or subscribe to a list, follow these steps:

1. Pick a list.
2. Create a new email message and type in the appropriate address, using "mailto:" if you are in your browser, and deleting it if you are already in your email window.
3. Leave your subject line blank.
4. In the body of the message, type: **subscribe <Name of List> <Your Name>.**
5. Send the message. You will be automatically added to the subscriber list and begin receiving posts in your email within a few hours. You will receive a welcome message. Keep this message because it contains important information, such as guidelines for subscribers, how to send messages to the list, and how to leave the list.
6. To subscribe to other lists, simply replace the listserv name with any of the mailing list names below.

Other Educational Mailing Lists

AASNET-L   African American Student Network.
                     mailto:listserv@listserv.uh.edu

ACIMEG   Computer hardware/software for music teaching and learning.
                     mailto:listserv@deakin.oz.au

ACSOFT-L   Educational software discussion.
                     mailto:listserv@wuvmd.wustl.edu

ADLTED-L   Canada-based adult education list.
                     mailto:listserv@ureginal.uregina.ca

ADMIN.	Educational Administration discussion.
	mailto:listproc@bgu.edu
AEDNET.	Adult Education discussion.
	mailto:listserv@alpha.acast.nova.edu
AEMA–L.	Arizona Educational Media Assoc. list.
	mailto:listserv@asuvm.inre.asu.edu
AERA.	The American Educational Research Association runs the following sublists at:
	mailto:listserv@asu.edu
AERA–GSL.	Graduate Studies List (faculty, admin and students)
AERA–A.	Educational Administration Forum
AERA–B.	Curriculum Studies Forum
AERA–C.	Learning and Instruction
AERA–D.	Measurement and Research Methodology
AERA–E.	Counseling and Human Development
AERA–F.	History and Historiography
AERA–G.	Social Context of Education
AERA–H.	School Evaluation and Program Development
AERA–I.	Education in the Professions
AERA–J.	Postsecondary Education
AERA–K.	Teaching and Teacher Education
ALF–L.	Academic Librarian's Forum list.
	mailto:listserv@vm1.yorku.ca
ALTLEARN.	Alternative approaches to learning discussion.
	mailto:listserv@sjuvm.stjohns.edu
AMTEC.	Media and technology in education.
	mailto:listproc@camosun.bc.ca
ASAT–EVA.	Distance learning discussion.
	mailto:listserv@unlvm.unl.edu
ASDEN.	Australian Schools of Distance Education Network (K-12) list.
	mailto:majordomo@cleo.murdoch.edu.au
AUDIOGRAPHICS–L.	Audiographics in distance education.
	mailto:listserv@cln.etc.bc.ca
BGEDU–L.	Educator's forum on reform.
	mailto:bgedu-l@ukcc.uky.edu

BILINGUE-L.   Developmental bilingual elementary education list.
                               mailto:listserv@Reynolds.k12.or.us

BIOPI-L.   Biology and education discussion.
                               mailto:listserv@ksuvm.ksu.edu

BIRTH-THREE.   Discussion for early childhood professionals.
                               mailto:majordomo@ngus.mystery.com

BULLY-L.   Bullying and victimization in schools list.
                               mailto:listserv@nic.surfnet.nl.

CAERLEON.   Hands-on history teaching discussion.
                               mailto:listproc@u.washington.edu

CALIBK12.   California K-12 librarians discussion.
                               mailto:listserv@sjsuvm1.sjsu.edu

CARET.   Capital Area Researchers in Educational Technology Discussion List.
                               mailto:listserv@gwuvm.gwu.edu

C-EDRES.   Discussion of online educational resources.
                               mailto:c-edres-server@unb.ca

CESNEWS.   Coalition of Essential Schools News.
                               mailto:listserv@brownvm.brown.edu

CHARTERSCHOOLS.   Charter school discussion list.
                               mailto:listserv@listserv.syr.edu

CHATBACK.   Special education discussion.
                               mailto:listserv@sjuvm.stjohns.edu

CHILDRENS-VOICE.   Publishes writing from children ages 5-14.
                               mailto:listproc@scholnet.carleton.ca

CMC-SIG.   Computer Mediated Communication list.
                               mailto:listserv@deakin.edu.au

CNEDUC-L.   Computer networking in education discussion.
                               mailto:listserv@tamvm1.tamu.edu

COLICDE.   Distance education research bulletin.
                               mailto:colicde-request@unixg.ubc.ca

COMMCOLL.   Community college discussion.
                               mailto:listserv@ukcc.uky.edu

COSNDISC.	COSN discussion list. **mailto:listproc@yukon.cren.org**
CPI-L.	List concerning the College Preparatory Initiative. **mailto:listserv@cunyvm.cuny.edu**
CREAD-D.	Distance education quality control discussion. **mailto:listserv@vm1.yorku.ca**
CREWRT-L.	Creative Writing in Education for Teachers and Students list. **mailto:listproc@lists.missouri.edu**
CSHCN-L.	Children with special health care needs list. **mailto:listserv@nervm.nerdc.ufl.edu**
DECTEI-L.	DEC's Education Initiative List. **mailto:listserv@ubvm.cc.buffalo.edu**
DEOS-L.	Distance Education On-line symposium of the American Center for the Study of Distance Education (ACSDE). **mailto:listserv@psuvm.psu.edu**
DEOSNEWS.	Distribution list for the monthly ACSDE Electronic Journal. **mailto:listserv@psuvm.psu.edu**
DISTED.	Discussion on distance education. **mailto:listserv@uwavm.u.washington.edu**
DRUGABUS.	Drug abuse education list. **mailto:listserv@umab.umd.edu**
DTS-L.	Dead Teacher's Society List, a broad education discussion. **mailto:listserv@iubvm.ucs.indiana.edu**
ECENET-L.	Early childhood education list. **mailto:listserv@postoffice.cso.uiuc.edu**
ECEOL-L.	Early Childhood Education On-Line mailing list. **mailto:listserv@maine.maine.edu**
ECID-L.	Educational Computing and Instructional Development. **mailto:listserv@vm.cc.purdue.edu**
EDAD-L.	Educational Administration Discussion List. **mailto:listserv@wvnvm.wvnet.edu**
EDINFO.	Updates from the U.S. Department of Education. **mailto:listproc@inet.ed.gov**

EDISTA.   Educacion a Distancia (in Spanish).
                        mailto:listserv@usachvm1.usach.cl

EDLAW.   Legal issues in education.
                        mailto:listserv@ukcc.uky.edu

EDNET.   Discussion of education and networking.
                        mailto:listserv@lists.umass.edu

EDNETNY.   Educational Development Network of New York.
                        mailto:listserv@suvm.syr.edu

EDPHIL.   Educational philosophy discussion.
                        mailto:listproc2@bgu.edu

EDPOL.   Education policy discussion.
                        mailto:listproc@wais.com

EDPOLICY.   Educational policy analysis.
                        mailto:listserv@asuvm.inre.asu.edu

EDPOLYAR.   Educational policy analysis archive.
                        mailto:listserv@asuvm.inre.asu.edu

EDSTYLE.   Discussion of educational styles.
                        mailto:listserv@sjuvm.stjohns.edu

EDTECH.   Education and technology list.
                        mailto:listserv@msu.edu

EDTECPOL.   Conference on Educational Technology Policy.
                        mailto:listserv@umdd.umd.edu

EDUCAI-L.   Discussion of artificial intelligence in education.
                        mailto:listserv@wvnvm.wvnet.edu

EDUTEL.   Education and technology list.
                        mailto:listserv@vm.its.rpi.edu

EFFSCHPRAC.   Effective school practices list.
                        mailto:mailserv@oregon.uoregon.edu

EJCREC.   Electronic Journal of Communications.
                        mailto:comserve@vm.its.rpi.edu
                        Use "join" instead of "subscribe" when signing up for this list.

EKIDS.   Electronic Kids Internet Server list.
                        mailto:majordomo@citybeach.wa.edu.au

ELEASAI.	Library and information science research e-conference. **mailto:listserv@arizvm1.ccit.arizona.edu**
ELED-L.	Elementary Education list. **mailto:listserv@ksuvm.ksu.edu**
ELEMUG.	Elementary School Users' Group. **mailto:listserv@uicvm.uic.edu**
ENVILIT.	Environmental literacy discussion. **mailto:listproc@listproc.wsu.edu**
ESPAN-L.	Teaching Spanish literature and language list. **mailto:listserv@taunivm.tau.ac.il**
EST-L.	Teachers of English for Science and Technology. **mailto:listserv@asuvm.inre.asu.edu**
ETCC-L.	Educational Technology Coordinating Committee. **mailto:listserv@admin.humberc.on.ca**
EUITLIST.	Educational uses of information technology. **mailto:euitlist@bitnic.educom.edu**
FLAC-L.	Foreign language across the curriculum. **mailto:listserv@brownvm.brown.edu**
FLASC-L.	Foreign language program coordination. **mailto:listserv@uci.edu**
FLTEACH.	Foreign Language Teaching Forum. **mailto:listserv@ubvm.cc.buffalo.edu**
GENTALK.	Teacher/student discussion of genetics and bioethics. **mailto:listserv@usa.net**
GEOGED.	Geography education list. **mailto:listserv@ukcc.uky.edu**
GLOBAL_ED.	Global education discussion. **mailto:global_edrequest@bbs68.nanaimo.bc.ca**
GRANTS-L.	NSF grants information list. **mailto:listserv@jhuvm.hcf.jhu.edu**
HOME-ED.	Home schooling discussion. **mailto:majordomo@world.std.com**

HOME-ED-POLITICS. Political subjects in home education list.
mailto:listproc@Mainstream.net

HOMESCHOOL. Home schooling discussion.
mailto:majordomo@efn.org

HORIZON. Discussion of the *On The Horizon* education journal.
mailto:listserv@unc.edu

HORIZONS. Adult Education journal.
mailto:listserv@alpha.acast.nova.edu

INSEA-L. International Society for Education Through Art.
mailto:listserv@unbvm1.csd.unb.ca

INTER-L. Internet in education discussion.
mailto:listproc2@bgu.edu

ITD-TOC. Information and technology for the disabled journal.
mailto:listserv@sjuvm.stjohns.edu

ITFS-L. Instructional TV Fixed Service discussion.
mailto:listserv@enm.uma.maine.edu

ITTE. Discussion on information technology and teacher education.
mailto:listserv@deakin.oz.au

JEI-L. Discussion of technology (especially CD-ROM) in K-12.
mailto:listserv@umdd.umd.edu

JTE-L. Journal of Technology Education.
mailto:listserv@vtvm1.cc.vt.edu

KIDCAFE. Kid's discussion group.
mailto:listserv@vm1.nodak.edu

KIDINTRO. Penpal group for children.
mailto:listserv@sjuvm.stjohns.edu

KIDS-ACT. Activity projects for kids.
mailto:listserv@vm1.nodak.edu

K12ADMIN. Discussions concerning educational administration.
mailto:listserv@listserv.syr.edu

K12-AUP. Acceptable Use Policies discussion.
mailto:k12-aup-request@merit.edu
Type "subscribe" in body of message.

L-ACLRNG.
Active and collaborative learning list.
mailto:listserv@psuvm.psu.edu

LEARN-NET.
Discussion for new Internet users.
mailto:learn-net-request@iastate.edu
Your message should say "subscribe" and nothing else.

LM_NET.
Library media specialist information exchange.
mailto:listserv@listserv.syr.edu

LRNASST.
Learning assistance issues.
mailto:listserv@arizvm1.ccit.arizona.edu

LRN-ED.
Support and information for K-12 teachers.
mailto:listserv@suvm.syr.edu

MATHEDCC.
Technology in math education discussion.
mailto:listserv@vm1.mcgill.ca

MATHSED-L.
Discussion group on Mathematics in Education.
mailto:listserv@deakin.edu.au

MDK-12.
K-12 teachers in Maryland discussion.
mailto:listserv@umdd.umd.edu

MEDIA-L.
Discussion of media in education.
mailto:listserv@bingvmb.cc.binghamton.edu

MEDIA-L.
Discussion of media literacy.
mailto:listserv@nmsu.edu

MEMO-NET.
Educational media discussion.
mailto:listserv@vax1.mankato.msus.edu

MEMORIES.
Allows kids to talk with WWII survivors.
mailto:listserv@sjuvm.stjohns.edu

MULT-ED.
Multicultural education list.
mailto:listproc@gmu.edu

MULTIAGE.
Multiple age schooling list.
mailto:listproc@services.dese.state.mo.us

MULTC-ED.
Multicultural education discussion.
mailto:listserv@umdd.umd.edu

MULTICULTURAL-ED.
Multicultural education list.
mailto:listproc@lists.fsu.edu

MULTI-L.   Discussion of multilingual education.
                  mailto:listserv@barilvm.biu.ac.il

MULTI-MEDIA.   Multi-Media Discussion.
                  mailto:listserv@deakin.edu.au

MUSIC-ED.   Music education discussion.
                  mailto:listserv@artsedge.kennedy-center.org

MY-VIEW.   A global creative writing exchange for kids.
                  mailto:listserv@sjuvm.stjohns.edu

NAEATASK.   NAEA Art Teacher Education Task Force list.
                  mailto:listserv@arizvm1.ccit.arizona.edu

NAT-EDU.   K-12 Education and Indigenous Peoples group.
                  mailto:listserv@indycms.iupui.edu

NCPRSE-L.   Discussion of science education reform.
                  mailto:listserv@ecuvm.cis.ecu.edu

NETWORK-NUGGETS-L. Online education resources list.
                  mailto:listproc@cln.etc.bc.ca

NEWEDU-L.   New patterns in education list.
                  mailto:listserv@uhccvm.uhcc.hawaii.edu

NLA.   National Literacy Advocacy list.
                  mailto:majordomo@world.std.com

NOVAE.   Teachers and networking list.
                  mailto:listserv@idbsu.idbsu.edu

OUTDOOR-ED.   Outdoor education list.
                  mailto:listserv@latrobe.edu.au

PARENTING-L.   Parenting issues list.
                  mailto:listserv@postoffice.cso.uiuc.edu

PENPAL-L.   Online penpal exchange.
                  mailto:listserv@unccvm.uncc.edu

PERKACT.   Discussion of the Perkins Vocational Education Act.
                  mailto:listserv@siuvmb.siu.edu

PHILOSED.   Philosophy of education discussion.
                  mailto:sued@syr.edu

PHYSHARE.   High school physics resources list.
mailto:listserv@psuvm.psu.edu

PHYS-L.   Physics educators list.
mailto:listproc@atlantis.cc.uwf.edu

PHYS-STU.   Physics students list.
mailto:listserv@uwf.cc.uwf.edu

PMIC-PENGUIN.   International cultural discussion for students.
mailto:majordomo@hampstead.k12.nh.us

POLYED.   Discussion of issues related to teaching polymer chemistry.
mailto:listproc2@bgu.edu

PRINT-SIG.   Use of printed material in distance education.
mailto:listserv@deakin.edu.au

SATEDU-L.   Satellite education list.
RL: mailto:listserv@wcupa.edu

SCHOOL-L.   Discussion for primary and secondary schools.
mailto:listserv@irlearn.ucd.ie

SHED.   Secondary and higher ed discussion.
mailto:listserv@etsuadmn.etsu.edu

SIGTEL-L.   Discussion of telecommunications in education.
mailto:listproc@list.acs.ohio-state.edu

SLART-L.   Second language acquisition teaching.
mailto:listserv@cunyvm.cuny.edu

SNS-L.   Teaching native Spanish speakers list.
mailto:listproc@cornell.edu

SPOKVIS-SIG.   Spoken and visual communication in distance education.
mailto:listserv@deakin.edu.au

STARNET.   Students at risk discussion.
mailto:listproc@services.dese.state.mo.us

STLHE-L.   Teaching and learning in higher ed list.
mailto:listserv@unbvm1.csd.unb.ca

TAG-L.   Talented and gifted education discussion.
mailto:listserv@listserv.nodak.edu

TALKBACK.

News exchange and discussion for kids.
mailto:listserv@sjuvm.stjohns.edu

TAMHA.

Teaching American History list.
mailto:listserv@cms.cc.wayne.edu

TAWL.

Teaching whole language discussion.
mailto:listserv@listserv.arizona.edu

TEACHEFT.

Teaching effectiveness discussion.
mailto:listserv@wcupa.edu

TESLK–12.

Teaching English as a Second Language in K–12.
mailto:listserv@cunyvm.cuny.edu

TIPS.

Teaching psychology science discussion.
mailto:listserv@fre.fsu.umd.edu

TORCH–D.

Jewish home schooling discussion.
mailto:listproc@shamash.org

TRDEV–AUS.

Training and Development list.
mailto:majordomo@cleo.murdoch.edu.au

TUTOR–L.

Discussion of the International Tutoring movement.
mailto:listserv@edie.cprost.sfu.ca

T321–L.

Teaching science in elementary schools list.
mailto:listserv@mizzou1.missouri.edu

UAARTED.

Art education discussion.
mailto:listserv@listserv.arizona.edu

UKERA–L.

Dialog on education reform policy making. Similar to BGEDU-L.
mailto:listserv@ukcc.uky.edu

UNSCHOOLING-LIST.

Interest-initiated home schooling.
mailto:connect@ecentral.com

VOCNET.

Vocational Education discussion.
mailto:listserv@cmsa.berkeley.edu

Usenet Newsgroups

Usenet newsgroups, or newsgroups, are like a giant bulletin board. Anyone can read or post an article to any of the more than 29,000 different groups. Unlike mailing lists, Net users don't have to subscribe to a newsgroup to read its posts, but their Internet service provider must allow them access to "read news."

The following list includes newsgroups of interest to educators of all kinds. If the school or Internet service provider's news server does not carry a group you are interested in, ask them to add it. These are publicly available, free newsgroups any Internet service provider can access. Some are moderated, meaning a person reads the posts before putting them on the network. However, most are not moderated, so choose newsgroups carefully if students will have access to them. While the newsgroups listed here are appropriate for schools, it's good practice to always scan news articles in a newsgroup before making it available to students. The most active general newsgroup for teachers is **k12.chat.teacher.**

Education—Higher, Academic

news:bit.listserv.ashe-l	Higher Education Policy and Research
news: bit.listserv.edpolyan	Professionals and Students Discuss Education
news: bit.listserv.lawsch-l	Law School Discussion
news:comp.edu	Computer science education
news:info.nsf.grants	NSF grant notes (Moderated)
news:misc.int-property	Discussion of intellectual property rights
news:misc.legal	Legalities and the ethics of law
news:sci.edu	The science of education

Education—Higher, Student

news:alt.folklore.college	Collegiate humor
news:alt.save.the.earth	Environmentalist causes
news:bit.listserv.psycgrad	Psychology Graduate Student Discussions
news:bit.listserv.sganet	Student Government Global Mail Network
news:soc.college	College, college activities, campus life
news:soc.college.grad	General issues related to graduate schools
news:soc.college.gradinfo	Information about graduate schools

Education—Instructional Media

news:alt.binaries.sounds.misc	Digitized sounds
news:alt.cable-tv	Discussion of cable television service
news:alt.cd-rom	Discussions of optical storage media
news:alt.dcom.telecom	Discussion of telecommunications technology
news:alt.education.distance	Learning over networks
news:alt.internet.access.wanted	Connecting to the Internet
news:alt.internet.services	Services available on the Internet

news:bit.general	Discussions Relating to BitNet and Usenet
news:bit.listserv.cw-email	Campus-wide email Discussion
news:bit.listserv.edtech	EDTECH—Educational Technology
news:bit.listserv.nettrain	Internet Trainers
news:bit.listserv.new-list	New Mailing List Announcements
news:comp.ai.edu	Artificial Intelligence Applications to Education
news:comp.edu.composition	Composition and computers
news:comp.edu.languages	Learning computer languages
news:comp.fonts	Typefonts—design, conversion, use
news:comp.graphics	Computer graphics, art, animation
news:comp.graphics.misc	Miscellaneous information about computer graphics
news:comp.graphics.visualization	Information on scientific visualization
news:comp.lang	Discussion of various computer languages
news:comp.multimedia	Interactive multimedia technologies
news:comp.org.eff.talk	Discussion of Electronic Frontier Foundation (EFF) goals, strategies
news:comp.periphs.scsi	Discussion of SCSI-based peripheral devices
news:comp.speech	Computer generated speech—hardware and software
news:comp.text.desktop	Technology and techniques of desktop publishing
news:rec.arts.books	Books of all genres and the publishing industry
news:rec.video.production	Professional video production
news:sci.cognitive	Perception, memory, judgment and reasoning
news:sci.edu	The science of education

Education—International

news:alt.culture.kerala	The culture of the Keralite people worldwide
news:alt.culture.tuva	Topics related to the Republic of Tuva
news:bit.listserv.euearn-l	Computers in Eastern Europe
news:bit.listserv.mideur-l	Middle Europe Discussion
news:bit.listserv.seasia-l	Southeast Asia Discussion
news:bit.listserv.slovak-l	Slovak Discussion
news:misc.news.southasia	News from Bangladesh, India, and Nepal
news:soc.culture.afghanistan	Discussion of the Afghan society
news:soc.culture.african	Discussions about Africa
news:soc.culture.arabic	Technological and cultural issues
news:soc.culture.asean	Association of Southeast Asian Nations
news:soc.culture.asian	Discussion about Asian countries
news:soc.culture.australian	Australian culture and society
news:soc.culture.bangladesh	Issues and discussion about Bangladesh

Education—International (continued)

news:soc.culture.bosna-herzgvna	Bosnia-Herzegovina culture and society
news:soc.culture.brazil	People and country of Brazil
news:soc.culture.british	Britain and people of British descent
news:soc.culture.bulgaria	Discussing Bulgarian society
news:soc.culture.canada	Discussions of Canada and its people
news:soc.culture.caribbean	Life in the Caribbean
news:soc.culture.celtic	Irish, Scottish, Breton, Cornish, and Welsh
news:soc.culture.china	About China and Chinese culture
news:soc.culture.croatia	Croatian peoples and culture
news:soc.culture.czecho-slovak	Bohemian, Slovak, and Moravian life
news:soc.culture.europe	All aspects of European society
news:soc.culture.filipino	Group about the Filipino culture
news:soc.culture.french	French culture, history, related discussions
news:soc.culture.german	Discussions about German culture and history
news:soc.culture.greek	Group about Greeks
news:soc.culture.hongkong	Discussions pertaining to Hong Kong
news:soc.culture.indian	India and things Indian
news:soc.culture.iranian	Iran and things Iranian/Persian
news:soc.culture.italian	The Italian people and their culture
news:soc.culture.japan	Everything Japanese, except Japanese language
news:soc.culture.korean	Discussions about Korea and things Korean
news:soc.culture.latin-america	Topics about Latin America
news:soc.culture.lebanon	Discussion about things Lebanese
news:soc.culture.magyar	The Hungarian people and their culture
news:soc.culture.mexican	Discussion of Mexico's society
news:soc.culture.misc	Group for discussion about other cultures
news:soc.culture.nepal	People and things in and from Nepal
news:soc.culture.netherlands	People from the Netherlands and Belgium
news:soc.culture.new-zealand	Discussion of topics related to New Zealand
news:soc.culture.nordic	Discussion about culture in North Europe
news:soc.culture.pakistan	Topics of discussion about Pakistan
news:soc.culture.polish	Polish culture, past, and politics
news:soc.culture.portuguese	Discussion of the people of Portugal
news:soc.culture.romanian	Discussion of Romanian and Moldavian people
news:soc.culture.soviet	Topics relating to Russian or Soviet culture
news:soc.culture.spain	Culture on the Iberian peninsula
news:soc.culture.sri-lanka	Things and people from Sri Lanka
news:soc.culture.taiwan	Discussion about things Taiwanese
news:soc.culture.tamil	Tamil language, history, and culture

news:soc.culture.thai	Thai people and their culture
news:soc.culture.turkish	Discussion about things Turkish
news:soc.culture.vietnamese	Issues and discussions of Vietnamese culture
news:soc.culture.yugoslavia	Discussions of Yugoslavia and its people
news:talk.politics.china	Political issues related to China
news:talk.politics.mideast	Debate over Middle Eastern events
news:talk.politics.soviet	Soviet politics, domestic and foreign

Education—K12

news:alt.child-support	Raising children in a split family
news:alt.education	General discussion of education
news:alt.education.alternative	Charter schools, private schools, etc.
news:alt.kids-talk	A place for the pre-college set on the Net
news:alt.kids-talk.penpals	A place where kids can find penpals
news:alt.parents-teens	Discussions about raising teenagers
news:bit.listserv.edusig-l	EDUSIG Discussions
news:k12	General K-12 education discussion
news:k12.chat.elementary	Informal discussion for grades K-5
news:k12.chat.junior	Informal discussion for grades 6-8
news:k12.chat.senior	Informal discussion for high school students
news:k12.chat.teacher	Informal discussion for K–12 teachers
news:k12.ed	K-12 Education
news:k12.ed.art	Art curriculum
news:k12.ed.business	Business education curriculum
news:k12.ed.comp.literacy	Teaching computer literacy
news:k12.ed.health-pe	Health and Physical Education curriculum
news:k12.ed.life-skills	Home Economics and Career education
news:k12.ed.math	Mathematics curriculum
news:k12.ed.music	Music and Performing Arts curriculum
news:k12.ed.science	Science curriculum
news:k12.ed.soc-studies	Social Studies and History curriculum
news:k12.ed.special	Students with disabilities, special needs
news:k12.ed.tag	Talented and gifted students
news:k12.ed.tech	Industrial Arts and vocational education
news:k12.lang.art	Language Arts curriculum
news:k12.lang.deutsch-eng	Bilingual German practice with native speakers
news:k12.lang.esp-eng	Bilingual Spanish practice with native speakers
news:k12.lang.francais	Bilingual French practice with native speakers
news:k12.lang.japanese	Bilingual Japanese practice with native speakers
news:k12.lang.russian	Bilingual Russian practice with native speakers

Education—K12 (continued)

k12.library	K-12 library and media discussions
news:k12.news	The latest educational developments
news:misc.education	Discussion of the educational system
news:misc.education.home-school.misc	Almost anything about home-schooling
news:misc.education.language.english	Teaching English to speakers of other languages
news:misc.education.multimedia	Multimedia for education
news:misc.education.science	Issues related to science education
news:misc.kids	Children, their behavior and activities
news:nptn.teacher.jewish-ed	NPTN Jewish education
news:pnet.school.k-12	Discussion about K-12 education
news:pnet.school.k-5	Discussion about K-5 education
news:relcom.education	Education discussions.
news:schl.news.edupage	Educom's thrice weekly EDUPAGE Newsletter
news:schl.sig.ethics	Discuss character/ethics/morals education
news:schl.sig.satl-con	Satellite conferences with Secretary of Education

Education—Multicultural

news:alt.culture.us.asian-indian	Asian Indians in the U.S. and Canada
news:alt.discrimination	Quotas, affirmative action, bigotry, and persecution
news:alt.native	Issues for and about Native Americans
news:soc.culture.african.american	Discussions about Afro-American issues
news:soc.culture.asian.american	Discussion about Asian-Americans
news:soc.culture.intercultural	A discussion on the pros and cons of multiculturalism
news:soc.culture.jewish	Jewish culture and religion
news:soc.culture.misc	Discussion about other cultures
news:soc.culture.usa	Culture of the United States of America

Education—Special

news:alt.education.disabled	Learning experiences for the disabled
news:bit.listserv.autism	Autism and Developmental Disabilities
news:bit.listserv.deaf-l	Deaf List
news:bit.listserv.l-hcap	Handicap List (Moderated)
news:k12.ed.special	Students with disabilities, special needs
news:misc.handicap	Items about the handicapped and Education Arts

Arts

news:alt.artcom	Artistic Community, arts and communication
news:alt.binaries.pictures.fine-art	Fine-art binaries
news:alt.binaries.pictures.fine-art.digitized	Art from conventional media
news:alt.binaries.pictures.fine-art.graphics	Art created on computers
news:alt.binaries.pictures.fractals	Postings of fractal-pictures
news:alt.emusic	Ethnic, exotic, electronic, elaborate, etc., music
news:alt.exotic-music	Exotic music discussions
news:alt.fractals.pictures	Fractals in math, graphics, and art
news:alt.movies.visual-effects	Learn about the ins and outs of special effects
news:bit.listserv.allmusic	Discussions on all forms of Music
news:bit.listserv.cinema-l	Discussions on all forms of Cinema
news:bit.listserv.film-l	Filmmaking and reviews List
news:comp.music	Applications of computers in music research
news:rec.arts.comics	Comic books, graphic novels, sequential art
news:rec.arts.dance	All aspects of dance discussed
news:rec.arts.fine	Fine arts and artists
news:rec.arts.misc	Discussions about the arts not in other groups
news:rec.arts.movies	Discussions of movies and movie making
news:rec.arts.movies.reviews	Reviews of movies
news:rec.arts.theatre.misc	All aspects of stage work and theatre
news:rec.arts.tv	TV—its history, past and current shows
news:rec.music.classical	Discussion about classical music

Computers

news:alt.3d	Three-dimensional imaging
news:alt.comp.acad-freedom.news	Academic freedom—computers
news:alt.comp.acad-freedom.talk	Academic freedom issues—computers
news:alt.folklore.computers	Stories and anecdotes about computers
news:alt.religion.computers	People who believe computing is "real life"
news:bionet.software	Information about software for biology
news:bit.listserv.c+health	Computers and health
news:bit.listserv.cdromlan	CD-ROM on Local Area Networks
news:bit.listserv.edi-l	Electronic Data Interchange Issues
news:bit.listserv.ethics-l	Discussion of Ethics in Computing
news:bit.listserv.euearn-l	Computers in Eastern Europe
news:biz.comp.software	For the latest software news
news:comp.admin.policy	Discussions of site administration policies
news:comp.ai	Artificial intelligence discussions

Computers (continued)

news:comp.archives	Descriptions of public access archives
news:comp.databases	Database and data management
news:comp.dcom.telecom	Telecommunications digest
news:comp.doc	Archived public domain documentation
news:comp.edu	Discussion of computers and education
news:comp.human-factors	Issues related to human-computer interaction
news:comp.mail.misc	General discussions about computer email
news:comp.risks	Risks to public from computers and users
news:comp.simulation	Simulation methods, problems, uses
news:comp.sys.transputer	Machine translation research
news:comp.virus	Virus discussion list
news:info.ietf.isoc	Internet Society discussion
news:info.labmgr	Computer lab managers list
news:misc.books.technical	Discussion of books about technical topics
news:misc.legal.computing	Legal climate of the computing world
news:sci.comp-aided	Use of computers as tools in scientific research
news:sci.crypt	Different methods of data encryption
news:sci.image.processing	Scientific image processing and analysis
news:sci.virtual-worlds	Modeling the universe

Future Studies

news:alt.cyberspace	Cyberspace and how it should work
news:alt.sci.physics.new-theories	Scientific theories not found in journals
news:alt.society.futures	Events in technology affecting computing
news:bit.listserv.fnord-l	New Ways of Thinking List
news:comp.society.privacy	Effects of technology on privacy
news:rec.arts.sf.science	Aspects of Science Fiction (SF) science

Help

news:alt.algebra.help	Aid for those algebra-plagued students
news:alt.child-support	Raising children in a split family
news:alt.parents-teens	Discussions about raising teenagers
news:alt.school.homework.help	An online homework helper
news:alt.sexual.abuse.recovery	Helping others deal with trauma
news:comp.answers	Answers to basic computer, Internet questions
news:misc.answers	More answers to basic computer, Net questions
news:news.announce.conferences	Calls for papers and conference announcements
news:news.announce.important	General announcements of interest to all

news:news.announce.newgroups	Calls for newsgroups and announcements of same
news:news.announce.newusers	Explanatory postings for new users
news:news.groups	Discussions and lists of newsgroups
news:news.lists.misc	News-related statistics and lists
news:news.misc	Discussions of USENET itself
news:news.newusers.questions	Q and A for users new to the Usenet
news:news.software.readers	Discussion of software used to read newsgroups

History and Humanities

news:bit.listserv.c18-l	18th Century Interdisciplinary Discussion
news:k12.Ed.soc-studies	Social Studies and History curriculum in K–12
news:sci.classics	Studying classical history, languages, art and more
news:soc.history	Discussions of things historical
news:soc.history.war	Discussion of famous military expeditions
news:soc.history.what-if	Discussions of how history might have changed

Language—Communication Studies

news:alt.news-media	News media discussion and debate

Language—International

news:alt.chinese.text	General postings of Chinese in standard form
news:k12.lang.deutsch-eng	Bilingual German with native speakers
news:k12.lang.esp-eng	Bilingual Spanish with native speakers
news:k12.lang.francais	Bilingual French with native speakers
news:k12.lang.russian	Bilingual Russian with native speakers
news:sci.lang	Natural languages, communication, etc.
news:sci.lang.japan	Japanese language, spoken and written
news:soc.culture.esperanto	The neutral international language, Esperanto

Language—Linguistics

news:comp.editors	Topics related to computerized text editing
news:comp.text	Text processing issues and methods
news:sci.lang	Natural languages, communication

Language—Literature

news:alt.books	Authors and novels, fiction and nonfiction
news:alt.mythology	Understanding human nature through mythology
news:alt.postmodern	Postmodernism, semiotics, deconstruction, etc.

Language—Literature (continued)

news:bit.listserv.gutnberg	GUTENBERG Project Discussion List
news:bit.listserv.literary	Discussions about literature
news:rec.arts.books	Books of all genres and the publishing industry
news:rec.arts.books.childrens	Discussion of the children's book industry
news:rec.arts.poetry	Discussion of poets and poetry
news:rec.arts.sf.misc	Science fiction lovers' newsgroup

Language—Writing

news:alt.prose	Original writings, fictional and otherwise
news:alt.pulp	Paperback fiction, newsprint production discussion
news:alt.usage.english	English grammar, word usages, related topics
news:bit.listserv.words-l	English Language Discussion Group
news:comp.edu.composition	Writing instruction in computer-based classrooms
news:misc.writing	Discussion of writing in all of its forms
news:rec.arts.int-fiction	Discussions about interactive fiction
news:rec.arts.poems	For the posting of poems
news:rec.arts.prose	For the posting of stories

Library and Information Retrieval

news:bit.listserv.buslib-l	Business Library List
news:bit.listserv.cdromlan	CD-ROM on Local Area Networks
news:bit.listserv.circplus	Circulation Reserve and Related Library Issues
news:bit.listserv.cwis-l	Campus-Wide Information Systems
news:bit.listserv.govdoc-l	Discussion of Government Document Issues
news:bit.listserv.libref-l	Library Reference Issues
news:bit.listserv.libres	Library and Information Research List
news:bit.listserv.medlib-l	Medical Libraries Discussion List
news:bit.listserv.notabene	Nota Bene List
news:bit.listserv.notis-l	NOTIS/DOBIS Discussion group List
news:bit.listserv.pacs-l	Public-Access Computer System Forum
news:bit.listserv.slart-l	SLA Research and Teaching
news:comp.archives	Descriptions of public access archives
news:comp.archives.admin	Issues in computer archive administration
news:comp.infosystems	Any discussion about information systems
news:comp.internet.library	Discussing electronic libraries
news:k12.library	Discussing K-12 libraries
news:soc.libraries.talk	Discussing all aspects of libraries

Philosophy

news:alt.sci.physics.new-theories	Scientific theories not found in journals
news:bit.listserv.ethics-l	Discussion of Ethics in Computing
news:bit.listserv.fnord-l	New Ways of Thinking List
news:comp.ai.philosophy	Philosophical aspects of Artificial Intelligence
news:sci.logic	Logic—math, philosophy, and computational aspects
news:sci.philosophy.meta	Discussions within the scope of "MetaPhilosophy"
news:sci.philosophy.tech	Technical philosophy: math, science, logic
news:sci.skeptic	Skeptics discussing pseudo-science
news:talk.origins	Evolution versus creationism
news:talk.philosophy.misc	Philosophical musings on all topics
news:talk.religion.misc	Religious, ethical, and moral implications
news:talk.religion.newage	Esoteric and minority religions and philosophies

Science

news:alt.fractals	Fractals in math, graphics, and art
news:alt.sci.astro.aips	National Radio Astronomy Observatories' AIPS
news:bionet.agroforestry	Discussion of Agroforestry
news:bionet.announce	Announcements of interest to biologists
news:bionet.biology.computational	Computer and math applications
news:bionet.biology.tropical	Discussions about tropical biology
news:bionet.genome.chromosomes	Discussion of Chromosome 22
news:bionet.immunology	Discussions about research in immunology
news:bionet.info-theory	Discussions about biological information
news:bionet.jobs.offered	Scientific Job opportunities
news:bionet.journals.contents	Contents of biology journal publications
news:bionet.molbio.aging	Discussions of cellular and organismal aging
news:bionet.molbio.bio-matrix	Computer applications to biological databases
news:bionet.molbio.embldatabank	Information about the EMBL nucleic acid database
news:bionet.molbio.evolution	How genes and proteins have evolved
news:bionet.molbio.genbank	Information about the GenBank nucleic acid database
news:bionet.molbio.genbank.updates	Hot off the presses (Moderated)
news:bionet.molbio.gene-linkage	Discussions about genetic linkage analysis
news:bionet.molbio.genome-program	Discussion of Human Genome Project issues
news:bionet.molbio.hiv	The molecular biology of HIV
news:bionet.molbio.methds-reagnts	Requests for information and lab reagents
news:bionet.molbio.proteins	Research on proteins and protein databases
news:bionet.neuroscience	Research issues in the neurosciences
news:bionet.plants	Discussion about all aspects of plant biology

Science (continued)

news:bionet.population-bio	Discussions about population biology
news:bionet.sci-resources	Information about funding agencies
news:bionet.users.addresses	Who's who in Biology
news:bionet.women-in-bio	Women in Biology
news:bionet.xtallography	Discussions about protein crystallography
news:bit.listserv.frac-l	Fractal Discussion List
news:comp.theory	Theoretical Computer Science
news:comp.theory.cell-automata	Discussion on all aspects of cellular automata
news:comp.theory.dynamic-sys	Ergodic Theory and Dynamical Systems
news:comp.theory.info-retrieval	Information Retrieval topics
news:comp.theory.self-org-sys	Topics related to self-organization
news:info.nsf.grants	NSF grant notes
news:info.theorynt	Theory list
news:k12.ed.math	Mathematics curriculum in K–12
news:k12.ed.science	Science curriculum in K–12
news:sci.aeronautics	Science of aeronautics and related technology
news:sci.aquaria	Only scientifically oriented postings re: aquaria
news:sci.astro	Astronomy discussions and information
news:sci.astro.hubble	Processing Hubble Space Telescope data
news:sci.bio.misc	Biology and related sciences
news:sci.bio.technology	Any topic relating to biotechnology
news:sci.chem	Chemistry and related sciences
news:sci.comp-aided	Use of computers as tools in scientific research
news:sci.electronics.misc	Circuits, theory, electrons and discussions
news:sci.energy	Discussions about energy, science, and technology
news:sci.engr	Technical discussions about engineering tasks
news:sci.engr.biomed	Discussing the field of biomedical engineering
news:sci.engr.chem	All aspects of chemical engineering
news:sci.engr.civil	Topics related to civil engineering
news:sci.engr.mech	The field of mechanical engineering
news:sci.geo.geology	Discussion of solid earth sciences
news:sci.geo.meteorology	Discussion of meteorology and related topics
news:sci.logic	Logic—math, philosophy and computational aspects
news:sci.materials	All aspects of materials engineering
news:sci.math	Mathematical discussions and pursuits
news:sci.math.num-analysis	Numerical Analysis
news:sci.math.research	Discussion of current mathematical research
news:sci.math.stat	Statistics discussion
news:sci.math.symbolic	Symbolic algebra discussion

news:sci.med	Medicine and its related products and regulations
news:sci.med.aids	AIDS treatment, HIV pathology/biology, prevention
news:sci.med.physics	Issues of physics in medical testing/care
news:sci.misc	Short-lived discussion on subjects in the sciences
news:sci.nanotech	Self-reproducing molecular-scale machines
news:sci.optics	Discussion relating to the science of optics
news:sci.physics	Physical laws, properties
news:sci.physics.fusion	Information on fusion, especially "cold" fusion
news:sci.research	Research methods, funding, ethics, and whatever
news:sci.research.careers	Issues relevant to careers in scientific research
news:sci.space.news	Announcements of space-related news items
news:sci.space.policy	Space, space programs, space research
news:sci.space.shuttle	The space shuttle and the STS program

Science—Social

news:alt.folklore	Science of folklore
news:alt.folklore.urban	Urban legends
news:alt.society.civil-liberty	Civil Liberties Discussion
news:bit.listserv.qualrs-l	Qualitative Research of the Human Sciences
news:sci.anthropology	All aspects of studying humankind
news:sci.archaeology	Studying antiquities of the world
news:sci.cognitive	Perception, memory, judgment and reasoning
news:sci.econ	The science of economics
news:sci.edu	The science of education
news:sci.environment	Discussions about the environment and ecology
news:sci.psychology.misc	Topics related to psychology
news:soc.misc	Socially oriented topics not in other groups
news:soc.politics	Political problems, systems, solutions
news:talk.environment	State of the environment and what to do
news:talk.politics.misc	Political discussions and ravings of all kinds
news:talk.politics.theory	Theory of politics and political systems

Women's Studies

news:bionet.women-in-bio	Women in biology
news:soc.feminism	Discussion of feminism and feminist issues
news:soc.women	Women's issues, their problems and relationships
news:talk.rape	Discussions on stopping rape

World Wide Web Sites

The most exciting and easy-to-use Internet service is the World Wide Web, also called the Web or WWW. With the click of a button, students and educators can visit colorful Web pages packed with educational information of all kinds on computers all over the world.

The appeal of the Web over other Internet tools, besides its ease of use, is its multimedia capability. Besides accessing text and graphics, Web users can watch videos and listen to music or speeches. The Web's simple "point, click, and you're there" approach means users don't have to struggle with as many technical aspects of the Internet when they search for and retrieve information.

What follows is a tour of more than 50 of the best educational WWW sites on the Internet. Each snapshot includes a computer screen capture of the site, its URL address, and a brief description of its value to educators and students. They're in alphabetical order by name of site.

Armadillo

http://chico.rice.edu/armadillo/

Full of resources and instructional materials related to Texas, the Lone Star State. The content supports an interdisciplinary course of study with a Texas theme and includes hyperlinks to dozens of other Web and gopher servers related to education.

ArtsEdNet

http://www.artsednet.getty.edu

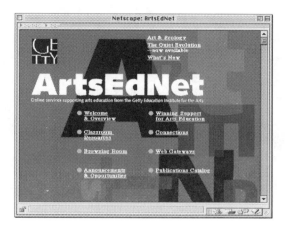

ArtsEdNet, developed by the Getty Center for Education, is a new electronic resource designed to support the needs of the K–12 arts education community. This expertly designed site includes departments such as Currents, where you'll find articles, news releases, and teaching trends and advocacy issues; Tools, which feature lesson plans and other curriculum materials; and the Library, which houses resources such as an image bank, and excerpts of various art education books.

Ask an Expert

http://www.askanexpert.com/askanexpert/

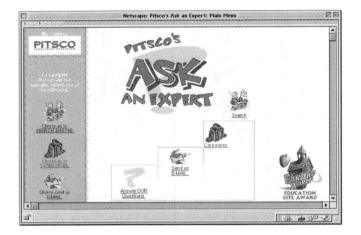

Astronauts, zookeepers, and writers from around the globe are all waiting to answer your students' questions about their careers — and you can find them all at this Web site! More than 250 experts are listed here, each one ready and willing to add their unique knowledge to your lesson plans, projects, and classroom activities.

Busy Teacher's K–12 Web Site

URL:http://www.ceismc.gatech.edu/BusyT/

This Web site is designed to provide K–12 educators with a direct source of online teaching materials, lesson plans, and classroom activities. It's also in existence to provide an enjoyable and rewarding experience for the teacher who is just learning to use the Internet.

Cells Alive

http://www.cellsalive.com

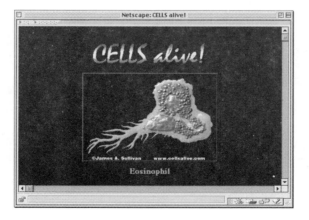

This "microscopy of living cells and organisms" site is packed with information and images of viruses, parasites, bacteria, and even "foodborne pathogenic microorganisms." Yuck! Uncover the truth about cryptosporidium parvum, which lurks in our water supplies, and discover how streptococci threaten white blood cells. After exploring the site, click on the link to Tom Terry's Microbiology Course, which contains short quizzes and tests related to the material.

Chetro Ketl Great Kiva

http://alishaw.sscf.ucsb.edu/anth/projects/great.kiva/

Students of Native American architecture, music, and artifacts will find lots to love about the Great Kiva Web site. This information-rich, easy-to-navigate site contains a three dimensional reconstruction of a Great Kiva, an architectural feature found in many prehistoric Anasazi communities in the Southwestern United States. Your students can take advantage of the latest technology to fly through the site in real time, as well as listen to period music, chants, and more.

Crayola Art Education

http://www.crayola.com/art_education/

Packed with engaging and unusual ideas, the Crayola Web site is an art teacher's dream, as it offers interesting uses for crayons, markers, finger paint, tempura, and clay. Also included is an Art Educator's Bulletin Board, where you can exchange lessons with other K–12 art teachers.

Dave's ESL Cafe

http://www.pacificnet.net/~sperling/index.html

Perhaps one of the best English as a Second Language Web sites around, Dave's ESL Cafe is chock full of useful ideas, activities, quotes, quizzes, and English idioms. Students with tough ESL questions can head over to the chat center, post their queries on the discussion board, or email them to ESL/EFL teachers from around the world — 24 hours a day, seven days a week.

Developing Educational Standards

http://putwest.boces.org/Standards.html

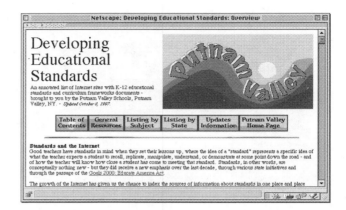

All educators have certain standards in mind when they create new lesson plans. While these standards are nothing new conceptually, lately they have received a new emphasis through dozens of state initiatives and through the passage of the Goals 2000 Educate America Act. This site has been created to help educators keep up to date with the latest educational standards information and contains more than 850 links to related information nationwide.

Dinosaur Exhibit

http://www.hcc.hawaii.edu/dinos/dinos.1.html

For the first time, people in Hawaii (and anywhere else) can visit a free, permanent exhibit of dinosaur fossils for public viewing — on the Web. Honolulu Community College gives K–12 students a look at the fossils of some of the largest creatures that ever lived, and even includes an audio tour. The fossils are replicas of the originals at the American Museum of Natural History in New York City, with one of the largest and finest collections of dinosaur fossils in the world.

Discovery Channel Online

http://www.discovery.com

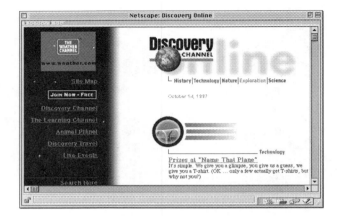

The Discovery Channel, known for its award-winning educational programming, now offers a Web site boasting original interactive content with film, music, photography, and illustration. Recent offerings include news bites with photographs of new species discovered in the Galapagos, information on Haiti's continuing political upheavals, and a guide to the cable channel's daily programming.

Education Place

http://www.eduplace.com

This rich site, sponsored by Houghton Mifflin, is loaded with curriculum materials for K-8 teachers. There's a math section, a reading/language arts section, a social studies area, and a technology center, as well as an activity search and project center. A great place to find some intriguing educational resources.

EDITOR'S CHOICE

Educational Resources and Information Center (ERIC)

http://ericir.syr.edu

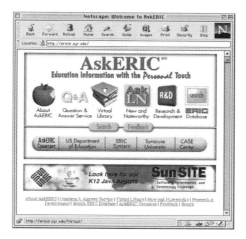

Sponsored by the U.S. Office of Educational Research and Improvement, ERIC is a one-stop source of the latest education information—from thousands of free lesson plans to full-text articles about K–12 education in the United States and abroad. The site is searchable by keyword. Email the staff for information on how to submit education-related Internet questions.

mailto:askeric@ericir.syr.edu

EdWeb

http://edweb.gsn.org

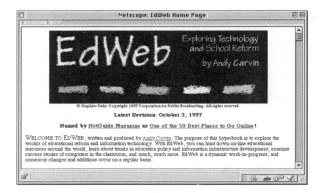

The purpose of this online "hyperbook" is to explore the worlds of educational reform and information technology. With EdWeb, you can hunt down online educational resources around the world, learn about trends in education policy and information infrastructure development, and examine success stories of computers in the classroom. EdWeb is a dynamic work-in-progress and is updated weekly.

Encyclopedia Britannica Online

http://www.eb.com

At 44 million words, the Encyclopedia Britannica is recognized as the world's most comprehensive reference. Now, advanced search and retrieval capabilities and hypertext linking via the WWW make this reference tool even more powerful. Britannica Online is a fully searchable and browsable collection of authoritative references, including Britannica's full encyclopedic database, Merriam-Webster's Collegiate Dictionary, the Britannica Book of the Year, and more. Visitors may try the site, but users who wish to make regular searches must pay a fee.

Exploratorium

http://www.exploratorium.edu

Housed within the Palace of Fine Arts in San Francisco, California, the Exploratorium is a collage of 650 interactive exhibits in science, art, and human perception. Students can explore many of them via this site. The exhibits fall into broad subject areas including light and color, sound, music, motion, animal behavior, electricity, heat and temperature, language, patterns, hearing, touch, vision, waves and resonance, and weather.

EDITOR'S CHOICE

Frog Dissection Kit

http://george.lbl.gov/ITG.hm.pg.docs/dissect/dissect.html

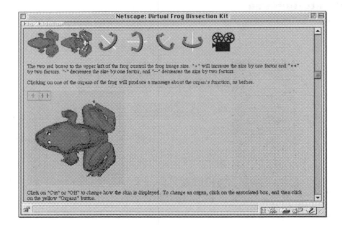

Designed for high school biology classes, this site allows students to explore the anatomy of a frog without dissecting a real animal. They can turn the frog over, remove skin, and highlight various organs and systems. Researchers used data from high-resolution imaging to create this one-of-a-kind site.

From Now On

http://fromnowon.org

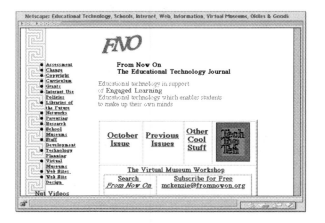

Written by veteran school Internet consultant Jamieson McKenzie, From Now On is an online publication whose time has come. Every month McKenzie addresses a hot button issue of interest to the wired K-12 crowd, outlining solutions with a very lucid, hands-on approach. Recent topics include "Protecting Our Children from the Internet and the World," "Creating Policies for Acceptable Use," "Creating Flexible Tech Plans for Individual Sites," and "Libraries of the Future."

Global SchoolNet Foundation

http://www.gsn.org

Global SchoolNet hosts nearly 100 innovative K–12 Internet projects each year, and continues to find innovative classroom applications for the Internet. You and your class can join in right away via this site. Their latest project involves connecting schools worldwide via inexpensive videoconferencing tools such as CU-SeeMe.

Grand Canyon National Park

http://www.kaibab.org

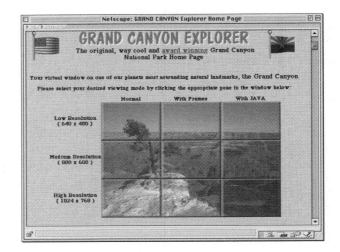

Take your class on a virtual tour of one of the most incredible places on earth. The Grand Canyon of the Colorado River is one of the seven natural wonders of the world and one our planet's most astounding natural sights. Hundreds of photos of wildlife and landmarks within the canyon await you.

Family Health

http://www.tcom.ohiou.edu/family-health.html

Students can use this site to listen to health information. It's an ideal opportunity for students with impaired vision to access the World Wide Web. Family Health is a daily, online series of 2.5-minute audio programs featuring practical, easy-to-understand answers to some of the most frequently asked questions about health and health care.

Homework Help

http://www.startribune.com/homework/

Created by the staff of the Star Tribune in Minneapolis, the Homework Helper Web site puts teachers in touch with students from all over the world to help them solve their homework dilemmas. Once inside the site, students are able to browse the questions and responses and post their own questions. Teachers monitor the discussions and post responses within 24 hours. These responses include enough guidance to help the student discover the answer to their homework problem on their own.

Hurricane Storm Science

http://falcon.miamisci.org/hurricane/

Developed with the elementary student and teacher in mind, youngsters can use this site to discover how hurricanes form and learn about weather instruments. Lots of fun and educational activities are provided, including "Andrew in 3D," where students view a Web image of Hurricane Andrew.

Intercultural E-Mail Classroom Connections (IECC)

http://www.stolaf.edu/network/iecc/

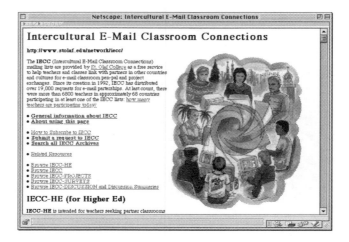

The IECC site is provided by St. Olaf College as a free service to help teachers and classes link with partners in other countries and cultures for keypal (online penpals) and project exchanges. A must for all educators.

Kidlink

http://www.kidlink.org

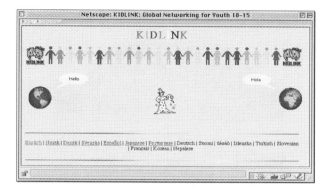

Kidlink is a grassroots project aimed at getting as many 10-15 year-olds as possible involved in a global dialog. Their work is supported by public conferences (mailing lists), a private network for interactive dialog (chat), and an online art exhibition site.

KidNews

http://www.kidnews.com

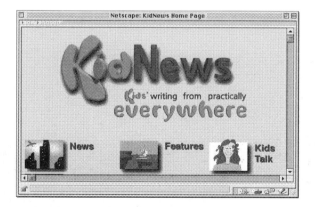

This site might be the best online forum for kids — well-designed, thoughtful, and child-friendly. There are a variety of forums that students can post to, from sports to current events. Visitors can contribute stories, poems, reviews, essays, or just look for pen pals. Writing contests are frequently posted as well.

Kindergarten Connection

http://www.kconnect.com

If you're looking for a site devoted entirely to kindergarten, make sure to check out Kindergarten Connection! This excellent Web site serves as an all-purpose guide for the kindergarten educator, serving teachers with lesson plans and reviews on kindergarten-based books. The lesson plans include your basic subjects, while stemming off into cooking and multicultural studies, all aimed at little rascals! Also featured is a teacher tips section, highlighting neat ideas for games like bingo and subjects such as math.

LD Online: Learning Disabilities Resources

http://ldonline.org

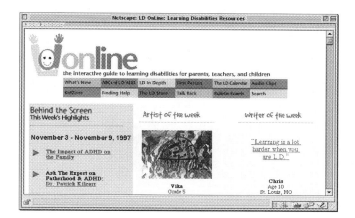

LD Online offers a tremendous amount of information on many different kinds of learning disabilities. The ABC's of LD provides visitors with a number of articles on types, causes, and determining learning disabilities. LD In-Depth has a large variety of topics such as math skills, ADD/ADHD, speech and language, and teaching techniques. The Kid Zone provides young learning disabled students with a place where they can play, learn and meet other people their age who have similar disabilities.

Letters from an Iowa Soldier in the Civil War

http://www.ucsc.edu/civil-war-letters/home.html

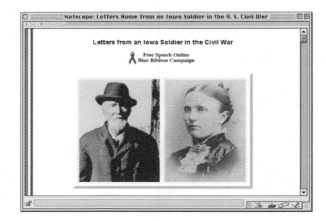

A valuable site for all students studying America's Civil War, the Letters from an Iowa Soldier in the Civil War site contains hundreds of letters and photographs. The site also includes portraits of Confederate and Union officers and enlisted men.

The Math Forum

http://forum.swarthmore.edu

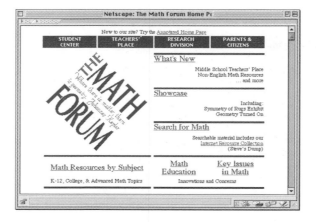

This excellent forum has something of value for everyone involved in mathematics, be they students, teachers, parents, professors, or those who just like math. There are sections on every topic of math, project ideas, search tools, links, and updates on key issues currently facing the mathematics community.

Mega Math

http://www.c3.lanl.gov/mega-math

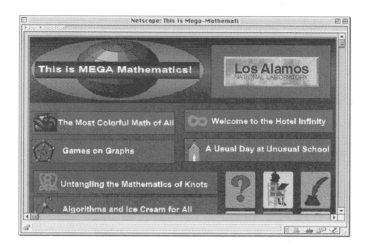

The Mega Math project brings some of the most unusual and important mathematical ideas to elementary school classrooms so young people and their teachers can think about them together. Each of the seven activities listed has an Activities and Evaluation page and covers subjects such as infinity, graphs, and algorithms. Easily one of the best math sites on the Web.

Microsoft Encarta Schoolhouse

http://www.encarta.msn.com/schoolhouse/

(continued)

This site is a rich, innovative online resource for K-12 educators worldwide. Every month the site features a timely curricular topic. Over the course of the month, the site's creators build an impressive collection of facts, links, and learning activities related to that topic. Your students can even have their questions answered by an expert in that field. There's also an impressive collection of interactive lesson plans created by other teachers, and a "lounge" area where you can explore information of interest to the educational community.

Music Education Online

http://www.wmht.org/trail/trail.htm

This page is designed to aid music educators in connecting with a variety of music education resources located on the Internet, as well as providing an interactive bulletin board for posting questions and comments on music. Of special note is the Lessons online area, where teachers can post their favorite activities or ask for help with a specific music-related problem.

National Aeronautics and Space Administration

http://www.nasa.gov

NASA operates dozens of Web sites of interest to educators. This new NASA home page is a one-stop link to all of them—from the Mars Explorer to incredible images from the Hubble Space Telescope.

National Archives and Records Administration

http://www.nara.gov

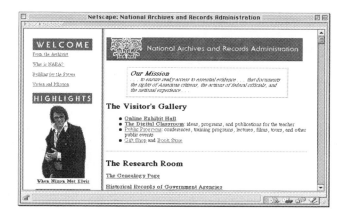

From this site, you and your students can access some of the most important U.S. documents ever to be produced, such as the Louisiana Purchase and the Emancipation Proclamation. The Digital Classroom section provides K-12 educators with materials from NARA, methods for teaching with primary sources, and sample lesson plans.

EDITOR'S CHOICE

National Geographic Online

http://www.nationalgeographic.com

This incredible, free online service gives you and your students access to exclusive national geographic content that's updated every day. Click on the variety of icons to link directly to content-rich articles, maps, geography quizzes, and more. Chat with Society photographers, writers, and artists, and exchange ideas with the leading scientific minds of our time.

Online Internet Institute (OII)

http://oii.org

Two leading online educators created the OII, which contains an impressive collection of professional develop-ment information for schools integrating the Internet and other computer technology into their curriculum.

Princeton Review

http://www.review.com

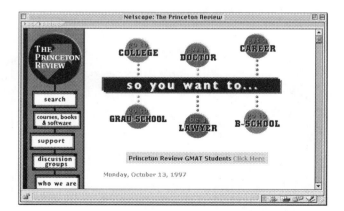

High school students can use this site to prepare for the SAT, GRE, and more! Each year, the Princeton Review helps more than 60,000 students get ready for college. The site includes rankings of the best colleges, and graduate, business, law, and medical schools, along with financial aid information.

Safe Kids Online

http://www.safekids.com

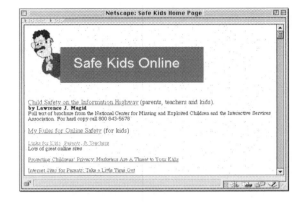

Internet-savvy educators have been aware for some time of the necessity of controlling student access to inappropriate material on the Internet. This important Web site outlines how to control student access to inappropriate Internet content, how to protect students' privacy online, and links to great, child-safe resources. An excellent resource for parents as well as teachers.

EDITOR'S CHOICE

Shakespeare Online

http://the-tech.mit.edu/Shakespeare.html

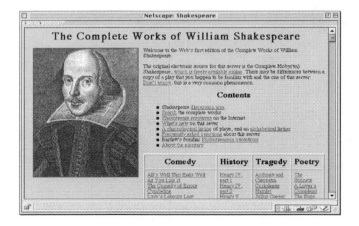

Shakespeare would be astounded to find his complete, annotated works available to anyone in the world via computer. Almost everything the Bard ever wrote is here, from All's Well That End's Well to poems like Venus and Adonis. Perhaps the best feature of the site is its hyperlink annotations, an essential aid in understanding the language of the time. A must visit for teachers and students studying the Swan of Avon.

Soviet Archives at the Library of Congress

http://sunsite.unc.edu/expo/soviet.exhibit/entrance.html

This exhibit is the first public display of the highly secret internal record of Soviet Communist rule. The legendary secretiveness and inaccessibility of the Soviet archival system was maintained through the Gorbachev era. The willingness of the new Russian Archival Committee to cooperate with the Library of Congress dramatizes the break that a newly democratic Russia is attempting to make with its Soviet past. Material long used for one-sided political combat has become fodder for shared historical investigation into the post–Cold War era.

Space Educators' Handbook

http://tommy.jsc.nasa.gov/~woodfill/SPACEED/SEHHTML/seh.html

Head over to this site to find space exploration movies, comics about the history of aviation, and an excellent section that teaches about space and science technology by using science fiction pulp novels and comic books to dispel popular myths about what's out there in the stars.

Teacher's Edition Online

http://www2.teachnet.com/index.html

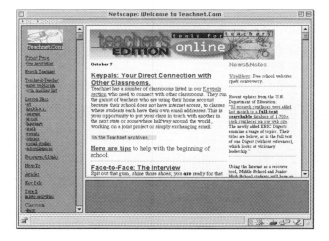

This site provides a forum for educators to network and share teaching strategies, knowledge, and wisdom. New hands-on information about classroom management, room ideas, organization, and public school relations is added daily. What's more, one new lesson plan and teaching tip is posted online every day of the school year!

Teachers Helping Teachers

http://pacificnet.net/~mandel/

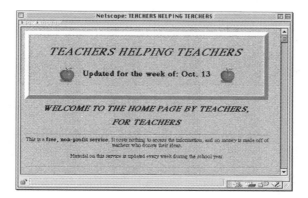

The goal of this innovative online service is to provide basic teaching tips to inexperienced teachers (ideas that can be immediately implemented into the classroom), new ideas in teaching methodologies for all teachers, and a forum for experienced teachers to share their expertise and tips with colleagues around the world.

Teaching with Electronic Technology

http://www.wam.umd.edu/~mlhall/teaching.html

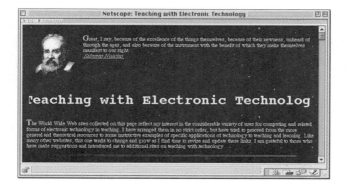

How can educators integrate the Internet into their curriculum, and then measure its affect on learning? This Web site provides the answers, with information about more than two dozen K-12 schools and institutions of higher learning already making the grade using the Net in the classroom. You'll find links to online courses and an online teaching demonstration using the Internet.

EDITOR'S CHOICE

TeleGarden Project

http://cwis.usc.edu/dept/garden/

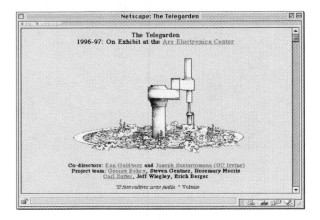

This telerobotic site allows students to view and interact with a California garden filled with living plants. Internet users can plant, water, and monitor the progress of the seedlings via the tender movements of an industrial robot arm. Your class can plant a seed in September and watch it grow over the course of a school year via the Net!

Theodore Tugboat Home Page

http://www.cochran.com/theodore/

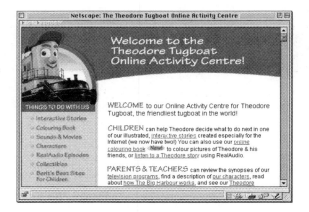

The online activity center for Theodore Tugboat, a TV show about a cheerful tugboat who likes to make friends and have adventures, will appeal to primary students. They can access an interactive story, retrieve a page from an online coloring book, and send themselves or a friend an electronic postcard with Theodore's picture.

Thomas Congressional Database

http://thomas.loc.gov

Through this site, named for Thomas Jefferson, the U.S. Congress offers access to the full text of just about all past and recent House and Senate bills, including summaries and chronologies of pending legislation; the Congressional Record, updated daily; email directories for House of Representatives and Senate members and committees; and C-SPAN transcripts and broadcast schedules. A valuable stop for educators and students studying the U.S. government and the legislative process.

The Virtual Study Tour

http://archpropplan.auckland.ac.nz/virtualtour/

Walk through the palace of Rameses III, or tour a Roman bath complex! This architectural site allows visitors to "walk through" computer reproductions of ancient buildings and modern structures. Click on directional buttons to move through the buildings as if you were really traveling through them. A fun, hands-on way to introduce students to the world of architecture.

Visible Human Project

http://www.nlm.nih.gov/research/visible/visible_human.html

The Visible Human Project has created a complete, anatomically detailed, three-dimensional representation of the male and female human body. The current phase of the project involves collecting CAT, MRI, and "cryosection" images of a male and female cadaver at one millimeter intervals. An interesting site for all secondary students and teachers of anatomy.

Volcano World

http://volcano.und.nodak.edu

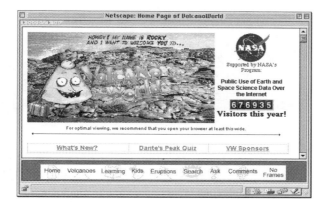

Perfect for students studying volcanos, NASA's Volcano World contains timely updates about volcanic activity worldwide, historical eruption reports, information on how volcanos work, and guidance on becoming a volcanologist.

Web66

http://web66.coled.umn.edu

Web66 is a one-stop source for all the software and information needed to set up a World Wide Web server at a school. Here you'll find the official Classroom Internet Server Cookbook, with recipes for setting up a WWW site on a Mac. It also includes Web66 SharePages, which are sample HTML pages you can download and use on your site, and several pages of pointers to Web-based resources appropriate for the K–12 classroom. These HTML pages can be used with any PC or Mac Web browser.

EDITOR'S CHOICE

WebMuseum

http://sunsite.unc.edu/wm/

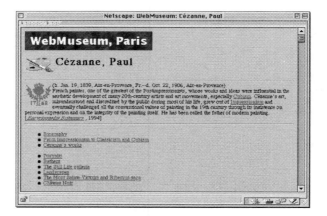

This online art museum, housing copies of some of the most famous paintings in the world, is free and open to the public 24 hours a day—no matter where you live! Visit the famous painting exhibition, a presentation of Paul Cezanne's works, and a medieval art exhibition. Students can also take a short tour of Paris or listen to a collection of classical music.

The White House

http://www.whitehouse.gov

An interactive citizens' handbook to the White House. Students can take an interactive, graphical tour, listen to recorded messages from the president and vice president (and Socks the cat!), and read a detailed account of family life at the White House. Internauts can even leave a message for the president in the virtual guest book.

The Why Files

http://whyfiles.news.wisc.edu

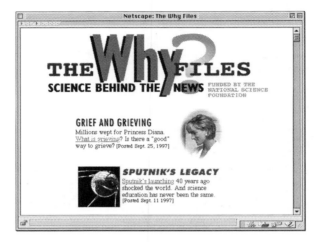

The Why Files, a project of the National Institute for Science Education, is an electronic exploration of the science behind the news. Twice a month you'll find new features on the science of everyday life. The site's boundaries are broad — from outer space to cellular biology, from dinosaurs and lizards to the statistics of political polling.

World Population Clock

http://www.census.gov/cgi-bin/ipc/popclockw

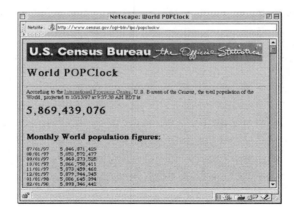

Students studying the continuing worldwide population explosion will find this site worth a visit. Updated once every ten minutes, the site provides an estimated count of the world population, along with facts and figures on how the numbers are calculated and an archive of past figures.

The Yuckiest Site on the Internet

http://www.nj.com/yucky/index.html

Have you got a burning question about some strange, puzzling, gross aspect of the world? Well then, this is the place to ask! Follow Wendell Worm as he takes you on a tour through some of the more icky areas of science. Learn about creepy cockroaches, wiggling worms, and that gunk that gets stuck in your eyes. Gross fun for the whole classroom.

HOW TO FIND THE INFORMATION YOU NEED QUICKLY AND EFFECTIVELY

Searching the Internet for information has never been easier, thanks to the Net's powerful online search tools. These tools, known as search engines and directories, are fast, easy to use, and, unlike the local library, are open 24 hours a day for you and your students.

Think of these engines as your school library's card catalog on steroids. If you've been on the Net, no doubt you've come across quite a few of these search engines with names ranging from Yahoo! to AltaVista.

This chapter offers reviews of some of the most powerful search engines and directories and shows you how to refine your searches so you're not perusing through thousands of links every time you enact a search. Each review gives you the inside information you need to decide whether that particular site is worth using to find the information you need.

You can reach all of the latest search tools by connecting to Classroom Connect's Searching Page.

http://www.classroom.com/classroom/search.html

Keeping It Simple with Directories

Nobody likes to do more work than they have to, which is why a directory should be your first stop when you need to find something on the Internet. Directories are sites you can visit that list thousands of other Internet sites organized by category, making it easy to click through and find what you want.

Stalwart souls at companies such as Yahoo! and Magellan make it their mission to collect the addresses of Web sites and organize them into categories that are easy for users to browse. Looking for social studies sites? Just go to Yahoo!, click on Education, then K-12, then Social Studies, and you'll find a concise list of links to quality social studies Web pages already organized so you don't have to search for that needle in a haystack.

Using Directories

To give you a feel for how directories work, we'll take you on a quick tour through one of the most popular ones, Yahoo!. Feel free to follow along on your computer if you want.

http://www.yahoo.com

1. Let's pretend we're looking for information on special education programs. We'll start out at the Yahoo! home page and click on the education link.

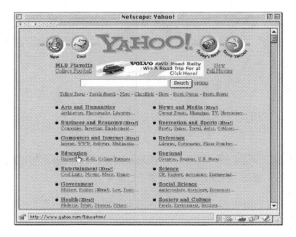

2. From there we're quickly sent to this page, a collection of links to a variety of Web sites dealing with education. Notice the **Special Education** link on the right. Let's click there and see what happens.

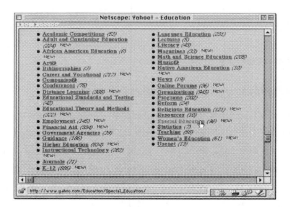

3. Here we are presented with a healthy list of Web sites — all dealing with special needs children! And next to each link is a brief description of the site, allowing us to peruse the list with a semi-critical eye. We're sure to find the information we're looking for at one of these sites, if not more. And it only took us a few minutes!

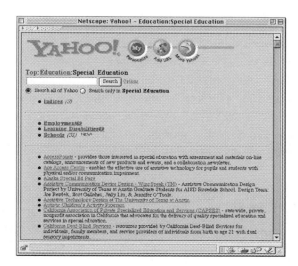

DIRECTORIES ON THE NET

In the unlikely event that we didn't find something helpful at Yahoo!, we could easily try one of the other directories on the Web — and there are quite a few to choose from. Below is a short list of some of the best online directories for K-12 educators. Check each one out, give it a test drive, and bookmark it if you find it useful. Note that some directories, like Magellan, include reviews of sites to save users time and effort.

Education World

http://www.education-world.com

Education World is a comprehensive online resource guide for K-12 education. Looking for online information on school projects or special education? No problem! Subjects at this site are arranged in an easy-to-read format to make finding the information you need trouble-free. Educational topics and index headings include administration resources, curriculum resources, vocational schools, K-12 schools online, and much more. Sites are given letter grades according to content, aesthetics, and organization. In addition, there's an online forum, lesson plans, featured articles by education experts, the latest education news, and employment listings.

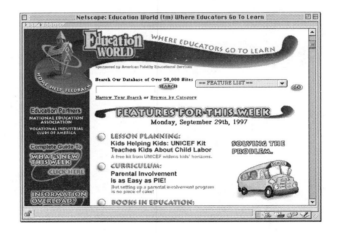

Lycos Top 5%

http://www.pointcom.com

The folks behind this site have taken it upon themselves to peruse the Web daily and decide which pages are the best of the best — the top 5% of the Web. (You may have noticed sites with Lycos' "5%" sign on their home pages.) Sites are rated according to their content, design, and overall enjoyment of the site on a scale of 1 to 100, with 100 being the highest. Best of all, each site comes with an extensive review explaining why the site is worth one's attention. Obviously, this site doesn't cover all subject areas, so don't use Lycos' index for an extensive search on a particular subject. Use it only if you feel like browsing or are looking for sites that are a cut above the rest.

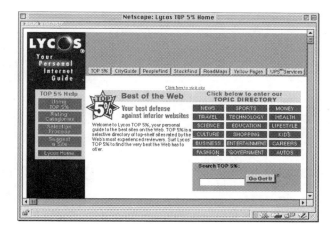

Magellan Internet Guide

http://www.mckinley.com

Magellan's writers review and rate thousands of new sites every month from every corner of the world. The listing for each site includes the name of the site, its rating, a partial or full description, and a link labeled "Review," which tells you the creator of the site, his or her email address, and Magellan's rating (one star being the lowest, four stars being the highest).

You can browse Magellan's categories, or you can use its powerful search engine, which connects you with a growing number of yet-to-be reviewed sites. This is an excellent directory for elementary teachers, as Magellan also reviews sites for inappropriate content. A site with a "Green Light" next to it means that it has been found to be free of "adult" material. Magellan isn't noted for its speed, so expect to wait a little for your search results.

Yahoo!

http://www.yahoo.com

Yahoo! is the directory that gets all the media attention, and with good reason. It's the largest and most popular directory on the Web. The categories are arranged in hierarchical order for easy searching. Unlike other directories, Yahoo!'s well-organized directory enables you to quickly track down quality information from its long lists. You can also enter your keywords into the search field to find specific information faster. Yahoo!'s popularity does have a down side, however. It can often take up to six months to add a new link, so it's usually a few months behind everyone else.

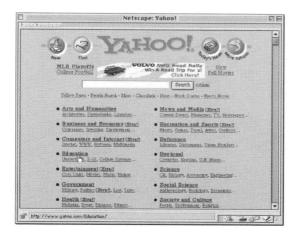

Yahooligans!

http://www.yahooligans.com

Yahooligans! is a searchable, browsable Internet index designed for Web surfers ages 8-14. Your younger students will find custom links designed to meet their unique needs, including hyperlinks to homework help sites, information about dinosaurs, and the latest kids news and weather reports. Yahooligan's information falls into eight broad categories — Around the World, Art Soup, Computers and Games Online, Entertainment, School Bell, Science and Oddities, Sports and Recreation, and the Scoop. Clicking on each of these brings up a list of subcategories until actual links appear. The creators have labeled their favorite sites with a "cool" icon, so it's easy to find the latest, most comprehensive Web sites in each area.

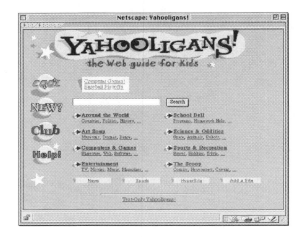

Other Worthwhile Online Directories

The Awesome Library — K-12 Education Directory

http://www.neat-schoolhouse.org/awesome.html

Blue Web'n Learning Sites Library

http://www.kn.pacbell.com/wired/bluewebn/

B.J. Pinchbeck's Homework Helper

http://tristate.pgh.net/~pinch13/index.html

Starting Point

http://www.stpt.com

Yeowsa! Educational Links

http://www.msjnet.edu:80/yeowsa/

Search Engines vs. Directories

Many people get directories and search engines confused. A directory is a man-made list of links you can browse, while a search engine is actually software backed up by lots of very powerful computers. Many large sites have search engines to help you quickly find specific information located on their sites. That's why many directories have search engines. Some sites, such as AltaVista, exist solely to provide you with access to their very powerful search engine software so you can quickly find what you need anywhere on the Internet — for free!

Searching the Net in a Flash with Keywords

The Net's search engines contain millions of up-to-date references to information that can be easily searched with keywords, a word or words that are used to find related documents or information on an Internet search tool. The Internet's search engines use these keywords to cut through the clutter in their databases of links and seek out specific references to the information you're looking for. This process of running a search takes anywhere from five to 30 seconds, after which the engines return the related links to you in an ordered listing.

The returns nearest the top most closely match what you've searched for; those near the bottom are less likely to be what you wanted, but still matched your keywords in one way or another.

In reality, the items near the top of the list received the most "hits" to your keywords, which means they received the highest score in terms of being the most relevant links to your search. (On the Net, searches are also known as queries.)

How Up-to-Date Is the Information in These Search Engines?

Very! Virtually all of the engines completely update their database of Net links once a month. That's quite a task, considering there are millions of computers for each of the engines to visit and millions of pages of information inside each computer to record and index.

Each search tool deploys thousands of Internet "spiders" to continually update themselves. These spiders crawl all over the Internet, visiting sites both old and new and recording what they find there. These records are quickly sent back to the search engine and added into its master index. It's this master index that you reference during an online search.

Which engines are the most up-to-date? The answer to that question changes monthly. Since each engine has spiders crawling all over the Net, each engine continually competes for the title of the largest index to the freshest Internet information. That's why it's important to use several search engines when doing your research. Don't rely on any one engine to find what you're looking for. Visiting three or four engines in turn will yield the best results.

Using a Search Engine

Search engines are incredibly easy to use and so fast you'll wonder how you got by without them in the past. Let's do a quick search of the Net using the AltaVista search engine to show you how it's done.

1. Load up your Internet browser and go to AltaVista's home page.

    http://www.altavista.digital.com

2. To search AltaVista's index to Internet information, enter your keywords into the blank box near the top. In this example, we'll do a search for the words **homework help math.** Remember that the more specific your keywords, the more likely the search results will include the material you need. Click **Search** or hit Return to begin searching.

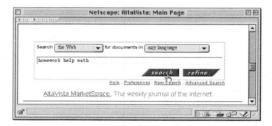

3. A few seconds later, the results appear. Take a look at the top of the results. In small type, you can see that the engine actually found about 342,920 documents that matched our query!

Thankfully, it only allows us to see the first ten results of our search first. That way we can scan through the first few hits to see whether we got what we wanted. Just follow each link by clicking on it. It'll take you to the site directly and allow you to view what's there. If you want to return to the search results, hit your browser's Back button a few times until you see it again.

If you aren't satisfied with the results, you can put new keywords in the search box, click **Search**, and see if you came closer to your goal.

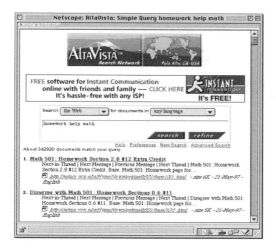

SEARCH ENGINE REVIEWS

Now that you know the basics of how to use an Internet search engine, it's time to review some of the best engines currently available online. Use these reviews to hunt down the search engines that will provide you with links to the information you're looking for — whether it's raw data, documents, graphics, software, or sound and video clips!

AltaVista

http://www.altavista.digital.com

Searching services offered: World Wide Web and Usenet newsgroup postings.

Description: AltaVista's enormous index is updated every four days, which means that your search results using this service will be fresher than most of the other search engines currently available. Also, the AltaVista searching engine is run on one of the fastest machines currently available from Digital, the company hosting the service. We tried eight different searches through the engine in the course of one day, and the results always came back in less than eight seconds. What's more, new improvements to the site allow you to refine your search more quickly and effectively than before, so you're sure to find what you need in a matter of minutes!

Search tips: Note that you have two option drag-down menus at the top of the screen. The first menu allows you to search either AltaVista's Web or Usenet newsgroup index for the keywords you enter into the search field. The second menu allows you to search in a variety of languages. If your search returns numbers in the thousands, clicking on the Refine button allows you to narrow your searches more effectively. From here you can even graph your search results to remove unnecessary phrases. You can also use the Advanced Search button to search by date, or construct carefully detailed searches that include (or exclude) any combination of words or phrases.

Deja News

http://www.dejanews.com

Searching services offered: Usenet newsgroup postings.

Description: Deja News is very fast, extremely comprehensive, and devoted exclusively to Usenet news-group postings. Reading postings through Deja News also gives you incredible flexibility, including the ability to click on the name of the person who's posted each message and send them email directly through your browser. All Internet users can post messages to Usenet groups, including thousands of experts in their field, and classrooms from around the world. If you're doing a long-term search, use Deja News to track down experts in the field you're studying. You have to be very specific with your keywords when using this service or your search results will be useless.

Search tips: Like most other search engines on the Net, DejaNews is strictly self-service. All you have to do is access the site, enter some keywords in the search field, and click Find. In addition to the regular search page, there is also a Power Search page for users who would like more advanced search options.

Excite

http://www.excite.com

Searching services offered: World Wide Web pages, more than 80,000 reviews of Web sites written by professional journalists, current news articles, and Usenet newsgroups (via Deja News).

Description: Very fast. Returns not only links to the information you're looking for, but rates each link by a 0-100% score (100% being the best) and a small description of where each link goes. The site also offers content in the form of news, weather, and stock information. Like many search engines, Excite is riddled with advertisements — some of them quite large, which will slow down your searches.

Search tips: Excite's technology offers a unique way to search the Web: by concept. What that means is that in addition to looking for the exact words that match your query, Excite also looks for ideas closely linked to the words in your query, allowing you to get very focused results in return. For example, if you searched for elderly people financial concerns, the search engine will find sites mentioning the economic status of retired people and the financial concerns of senior citizens, in addition to finding sites containing those exact words. If you find that one of the many results returned better describes what you are searching for, click on the words "More Like This" next to the URL. The search engine will then use that document as an example in a new search to find more sites similar to the one you liked. Head to the Power Search page or click on the Advanced Search link to refine your searches even more.

HotBot

http://www.hotbot.com

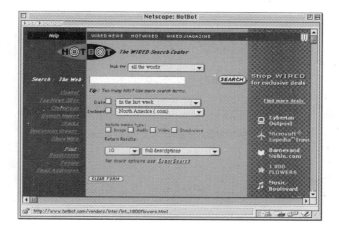

Searching services offered: World Wide Web pages, Usenet newsgroups, top news sites, classified, domain names, stocks, discussion groups, email addresses, and shareware.

Description: With more than 50 million online documents in its index, *Wired* magazine's HotBot is officially the most comprehensive Internet index! It's also the quickest search tool, returning most search queries in less than five seconds — right to your Internet browser screen, each returned link ready to be explored.

Search tips: HotBot's new interface allows users to refine their searches more than ever! With its pulldown menus and buttons, you can decide whether you want to search for an exact phrase, a title, a person, or just some of your keywords. You can also choose to search for information from the past two weeks or the past two years; whether you want to search sites from a specific continent, and how many return results you'd like to get back. For even more options, click on the Super Search link.

Infoseek

http://www.infoseek.com

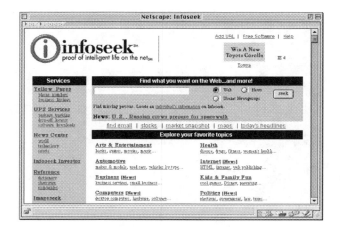

Searching services offered: World Wide Web pages, World news headlines, Usenet newsgroups, detailed information on over 45,000 leading public and private companies in the U.S.

Description: Infoseek offers a number of additional services, including a news center, UPS services, yellow pages, and a directory of more than 500,000 Web sites. The site's advanced search features allow you to search for a specific site, URL, title, or links to a page. No Boolean operators needed. When you do a keyword search, this feature provides you with both a list of the direct matches to your search and a set of closely related topics. Infoseek is also quick and returns links to both helpful and fresh online information. Infoseek also has built-in word stemming, meaning that when you search for a keyword such as quilt, it automatically looks for quilting, quilted, etc.

Search tips: Be sure to capitalize all proper names and locations. Use commas (,) to separate names and titles. Place double quotes (") around words that must appear next to each other in your search, as in "Renaissance art."

Lycos

http://www.lycos.com

Searching services offered: World Wide Web pages, World Wide Web site reviews, UPS files, personal home pages, Usenet newsgroups, image and sound files.

Description: Lycos offers quick searching of one of the largest Internet link indexes currently in existence. The Lycos catalogue is refreshed every three days. Search results include a useful abstract of the information found at each link, and, if available, a short review of the site. One of the best features of Lycos is that it has indexed millions of graphic images and free software available on ftp sites worldwide! You cannot perform a Boolean search, however. Nor can you search for combinations of words and phrases, and you can't view your search term in the context in which it was found.

Search tips: Doing a regular keyword search is a breeze. Enter your keywords, click Go Get It, and you're done. If you'd like to customize your search, click on the Lycos Pro link. This new section uses Java software to enable users to determine what's relevant to your search and what's not relevant.

WhoWhere

http://www.whowhere.com

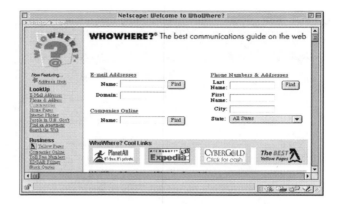

Searching services offered: Email addresses for Internet users worldwide; telephone numbers and postal addresses; personal home pages; and community searches.

Description: While WhoWhere does let visitors search the Web for information, its real power lies in its ability to help you find email addresses of your friends, organizations, and experts in thousands of fields — no matter where they live on the planet! Just type in part of their name or address, and WhoWhere does the rest. You can add your friends and family to the database with ease, thereby making it easy to find one another if you lost an address. WhoWhere also aids in gathering information on various companies and businesses.

Search tips: Essentially there are two functions provided: submitting a query, and performing an add or delete from the database. Adding a listing is free, although you do have to register with the service.

Similar sites:

411

http://www.four11.com

LookUp!

http://www.lookup.com/lookup/search.html

Switchboard

http://www.switchboard.com

Research-It!

http://www.itools.com/research-it/research-it.html

Searching services offered: Dictionary (English and computing), Thesaurus, Acronyms, Quotations, French and Japanese translators, french conjugator, anagrams, King James Bible searches, world map searches, CIA World Factbook search, U.S. area code and 800 number directory, global currency converter, stock quotes and symbols, zip code locator, and tracking of UPS and FedEx packages.

Description: Research-It offers access to so many helpful resources, it's absolutely incredible that they could assemble them all in one place. Each search tool is integrated right onto a single Web page. Just enter your search terms into each field for each tool, click Look It Up!, and the results appear a few seconds later. No advertisements. The site can take a while to initially download, however.

Search tips: Try them all, they're a blast!

Savvy Search

http://www.savvysearch.com/

Searching services offered: Links to more than a dozen other Internet search engines, which are searched in real-time. Sends keywords to Alta Vista, Excite, HotBot, Lycos, Yahoo!, and more!

Description: Savvy Search enables you to utilize multiple search engines at once to obtain the best results in the least time. Savvy Search is a meta-search tool designed to simultaneously send your query to multiple Internet search engines and return a complete set of results. It offers the advantage of a single location and common user interface for querying diverse databases. Your search may take several minutes, since Savvy Search accesses so many search engines. It is impossible to custom-tailor searches, since keywords are sent to each search engine simultaneously. Each engine has unique ways of customizing your search if accessed directly. Currently there is no option for case sensitivity or specification of words you do not want in your results.

Search tips: Enter keywords in the box labeled Query. This exact query is forwarded to the search engines queried by Savvy Search. Clicking on "Sources and Types of Information" will allow you to choose whether you want to search the entire Web, or just look for people, software, etc. Small words (the, it, for) are typically ignored. There is no need to insert "and" and "or" between words as this is done automatically.

Similar sites:

Internet Sleuth

http://www.isleuth.com/

Dogpile

http://www.dogpile.com/

MetaCrawler

http://www.metacrawler.com

Search.com

http://www.search.com

Shareware.com

http://www.shareware.com

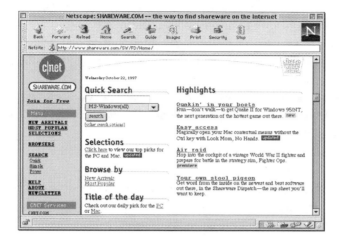

Searching services offered: Shareware.com offers searching through its index of nearly 200,000 Shareware software titles.

Description: If your lesson plans could benefit from using a piece of software (graphics, drawing, software calculator, etc.) then Shareware.com should be your first stop! It's easy to track down the software you need. Shareware isn't free software, however. Instead, each program's author expects you to pay for the program if you find it useful. However, feel free to use it for a few assignments, and if you want to keep it, then strongly consider paying for it.

Search tips: Select the kind of computer you use (platform), limit the files returned to 100, enter a search word, and click Start Search! A few seconds later, links to the software you are looking for are displayed. Click on each link to download the program right to your computer!

Similar sites:

Download.com

http://www.download.com

Jumbo

http://www.jumbo.com

Boolean Searching

Chances are you've probably done a few searches with the search engines reviewed above. You probably got several thousand results, but many were links to sites you didn't want. Don't be discouraged; this is a normal state of affairs for the beginning Internet explorer. Finding the information you want doesn't have to be a chore though, thanks to a little-known technique called Boolean searching.

There's not much to Boolean searching. It's simply a matter of using *and*, *or*, and *not*; two parentheses; a plus (+); and an asterisk (*) between and around the keywords in your searches. These words and characters are known as Boolean operators.

For instance, placing the word *and* between multiple keywords is a good first step in narrowing your quest, as it forces your search engine to look for information that contains all of your keywords, even if they're not right next to each other. For example:

industrial and pollution

biology and molecular

Search engines vary, but most assume that there's an *and* between your keywords even if you don't type it. Read the instructions for each engine to see how it handles this and other Boolean operators. Still, it doesn't hurt to type it between your keywords just to be on the safe side.

The *or* and *not* commands work in the same way, but with different results. For instance, typing

heaven or hell

will return any pages with either of those words, while typing

media not television

will return every page with the word media, but not the word television.

Be smart in choosing your keywords. For instance, here's a good Boolean search:

Cal or Ripkin and baseball and Orioles

Here's a bad search:

soviet or union

The first example will return dozens of links to the information you were looking for; the second will produce thousands of random hits with links to everything from the United Auto Workers Union to Lenin.

Putting quotes or parentheses around a set of keywords will force the engine to match the entire word or phrase as it stands. In addition, when you add a + after a phrase, followed immediately by a keyword, the search gets even more specific.

"carpal tunnel syndrome" +treatment

The quotes will force the engine to link the words carpal tunnel syndrome together exactly as they are and return links only to information that has the words all together, along with the word *treatment*. In other words, the phrase *carpal tunnel syndrome* must appear somewhere on the pages that are returned, along with the word *treatment* that can be found anywhere on the page. Think of the + as a super-powerful *and* — the word following the + must absolutely appear on the resulting pages.

If you put an asterisk at the end of a keyword, like bio*, the engine will look for every word on the site that begins with those three letters, whether it's biology or biography. This is called wildcard searching and can be very useful if you're not sure about the spelling of your keywords. It also works well when you're looking for root words with different endings. For instance, typing in quilt* will bring you sites with the words *quilt, quilts, quilting, quilted,* or *quilter.*

Note that using these operators may produce different responses depending upon the engine you're using. If you get some odd results, consult the engine's help screen or FAQ (Frequently Asked Questions) file for more information.

Other Searching Tips

- If you're in a hurry, AltaVista, HotBot, Savvy Search, and Yahoo! should be your first research stops on the Net. They're fast, up-to-date, and easy to use.

- Another tip if you're in a hurry — set the search tools to return the smallest number of results, say 10. This can usually be set using pull-down menus at each engine's home page. That way the search takes less time, and you still get a good sampling of the best results.

- Don't limit your search just to one area of the Internet. Be sure to use at least three of the engines to do a preliminary search. Time permitting, try others until you've found everything you need in a healthy list of sites containing the information you need.

- Capital letters in a search will usually force an exact case match. For instance, submitting a query for MacinTOSH will search only for matches of MacinTOSH.

- Some of the engines allow you to use the word *near* in your searches. Let's say you are doing a short biography on the life and times of Albert Einstein. Searching for Albert Einstein will turn up thousands of links related to his work, life, research, etc. To find documents related to his life, try searching for Albert near Einstein. (*Near* is sometimes called a proximity operator.)

- Don't get frustrated when you click on a search result and get some kind of an error. There are many reasons why this may have happened.

  - The Internet computer serving the information may be down at the moment.
  - Access restrictions may have been introduced at the server since the last time the engine indexed its information.
  - The server may be so overloaded that you can't get in for the moment. Try again in a few seconds!
  - You're Internet Service Provider or commercial online service may be having problems with their Internet lines. Call Technical Support if the problem persists.
  - The information may have been renamed or removed by its owner since the last time the engine indexed its information. (In which case, the site is probably gone for good.)

- Sometimes you'll go searching for something on the Net that you know is there, but the engines can't seem to find a link to it. There may be many reasons why this occurred.

  - Some servers specifically request that they not be visited by spiders from search engines, and most of the engines will respect that request.

- The page you are looking for is new. The engines are constantly searching the Net for new pages to add to their indexes, but it is likely that it will not find a brand new page (or a new version of an old page) for at least a few days.
- Sometimes an engine knows of the existence of a Web page because it has found a link to it, but every time it tries to retrieve the page to index it, the connection times out. This means there is heavy congestion at the server or the server is not online at that moment (meaning it probably crashed or went down for repairs/updates).
- The information is behind something called a **firewall.** Some information is stored on corporate Internet computers that are not publicly accessible, and the engines cannot access them. Likewise, any pages that require additional "work" beyond following a link (such as Web pages that require filling out a form, or registering, or providing a password) cannot be indexed.

Internet Integration 101

HOW TO BEGIN USING THE NET IN YOUR CURRICULUM RIGHT AWAY!

As school bells ring around the world, millions of teachers head to their classrooms with the Internet at their disposal. For the first time, these "Net newcomers" will experience the perils and the promise of the online world firsthand.

The promise? That you and your students can access up-to-the-minute information. Events that won't be documented in your textbooks for years can be explored on the Internet today. Your students can collaborate with peers and professionals located around the world and even invite electronic mentors to participate in your class projects — no matter where they live — in real time, with no delays!

Still, while the Net holds tremendous opportunities for enhancing the way teachers teach and students learn, it's an enormous, sometimes confusing place. It's one thing for a teacher to know how to navigate the Internet and find educational treasures — and quite another to be able to incorporate these treasures into the classroom in a meaningful way. Educators using the Net crave hands-on, step-by-step methods for integrating the online world into their curriculum, allowing them to fulfill their educational objectives while taking full advantage of online communication and navigation tools. But how can you use the Internet to its fullest in your classrooms, so that it becomes a part of your regular, day-to-day teaching activities?

The answer? Tightly integrate the Net into your curriculum by injecting online resources into your existing lesson plans. After all, the mere existence of the Internet doesn't suddenly mean that you should chuck all your old tried-and-true lesson plans out the window. Just the opposite. You can easily "Internet-ize" the same learning activities you have used in the past to energize your students and increase their love of learning, while helping you reach your educational goals faster and more efficiently.

Begin with Traditional Lesson Plans

The best way to start making the Internet a regular part of your curriculum is to add Internet components to your traditional lesson plans. Not every lesson plan works well with the Internet, though, so look carefully through your lesson collection for an activity you think will benefit the most from Net additions. While looking through your collection, remember: the best lesson plans do not use the Internet as an end in itself but employ it as a means to an end, incorporating its resources as an extra tool to attain a larger educational goal.

Good traditional plans that make great Net lessons include one or more of the following tasks*:

- **Comparing:** Recognizing the similarities and differences between items.
- **Constructing support:** Constructing a system of support or proof for an assertion.
- **Classifying:** Grouping things into definable categories on the basis of their attributes.
- **Inducing:** Inferring unknown generalizations or principles from observations or analysis.
- **Deducing:** Inferring unstated consequences and conditions from given principles and generalizations.
- **Analyzing errors:** Identifying and articulating errors in one's own or another's thinking.
- **Abstraction:** Identifying and articulating the underlying theme or general pattern of information.
- **Analyzing perspectives:** Identifying and articulating personal perspectives about issues.
- **Information gathering:** From human sources such as other students or subject matter experts.
- **Working in teams:** The Internet opens up a world of prospective collaborators for you and your students.

*Marzano, R. J., 1992. A different kind of classroom: Teaching with dimensions of learning. Alexandria, VA: Association for Supervision and Curriculum Development.

Once you've found one or two lesson plans that fall into one or more of these categories, log onto the Internet and begin looking for resources that can be included in each plan. Scout about for databases and opportunities to communicate with other students and experts in the fields you're researching.

Of course, the only way to *really* know if a plan is Net worthy is to get online and search for information on the subject. If you can find sites and resources that dovetail with the subject matter and goals of the lesson plan, then you're on your way to making it a truly valuable Internet experience for students.

While searching the Net, it's important to thoroughly explore the sites you plan to have students access. It's far better for you to uncover unpleasantries, dead ends, or inappropriate links *before* sending the class on an online mission. Avoid the temptation to totally abandon an Internet lesson plan because you can't find tons of information to fit into it. Some plans will succeed with just one or two Internet components.

Lesson Plan Sites on the Web

To get a handle on how other teachers have successfully integrated the Internet's resources and communication capabilities into their traditional lesson plans, visit the sites listed below. Your online time will serve two important needs: it will give you great ideas for how to bring the Net into your existing plans, and it will allow you to collect dozens of lessons developed by other educators for use in your classroom!

The Lesson Plan Page

http://libits.library.ualberta.ca/library_html/libraries/coutts/lessons.html

Teachnet.Com Lesson Ideas

http://www.teachnet.com/lesson.html

World School

http://www.wvaworldschool.org/

ERIC

http://ericir.syr.edu/Virtual/Lessons/
gopher://ericir.syr.edu:70/11/Lesson

Big Sky Lessons

gopher://bvsd.k12.co.us:70/11/Educational_Resources/Lesson_Plans/Big%20Sky

The Explorer Database

http://unite.ukans.edu

Communication Is the key

While you're busy tracking down lesson plan material on the Net, take some time out to network with other educators through Usenet newsgroups and educational mailing lists. These interactive meeting places are often frequented by experienced online educators who are more than willing to lend you a hand in your ongoing Net integration. Find out if anyone else has created an Internet lesson that's similar to the one you're trying to get off the ground. It may save you a considerable amount of time in the long run.

Also, keep your eyes peeled for teachers willing to share their lesson plans with you or who are willing to at least point you in the right direction. If you do ask others to help you out, be sure to post the final version of your lesson plan back to the list or newsgroup where you originally received help. This "giving back" has been occurring on the Net for years.

Give Them a Spin!

Once you've compiled enough relevant Internet resources to augment your lesson plan, the next step is to actually start writing your new, improved plan. How difficult this step will be depends on how much homework you have done up front.

It's fine to follow the same lesson plan structure or format as traditional plans, but you may get better results by starting from scratch. Print out your old plan and use it only as an outline. Start your new Internet plan with a blank word processing screen or a piece of paper, which often makes you look at the plan in a new light. You can still use the same basic template, but don't be afraid to rework and reorganize your new plan.

Once you've finished adding the Internet to a few of your lesson plans, have one of your Net-savvy peers give it the once-over. A fresh set of eyes, especially ones that are familiar with the Net, may see that you haven't allotted enough time or resources to your plan. It's easy to get wrapped up in the hunt for information and overlook minor but important details. Also consider doing a dry run of the plan to make sure that everything's in order.

If you do have a dry run (and you should), hold it at the time of day you'll be using the Internet and try connecting to your sites of choice. The Internet is busiest between 3 p.m. and 7 p.m. EST. If your lesson is scheduled during this time period, you may have trouble connecting to traffic-heavy sites. If so, you may have to be flexible with your site selections or schedules.

If you are using email for interpersonal communication in your lesson, keep time zones in mind. Setting up an exchange with a class or expert in Japan is wonderful, but remember what time it will be on their end when you're having your fourth period class.

Now all you need to do is give your new Internet lesson plan a try in the classroom. Bear in mind that like a regular lesson plan, it may not work as originally planned and may need minor adjustments to make it work better next time around. How will you know if your lesson was successful? Assess it the same way you would a traditional plan. If your students learned what you set out to teach, had fun, and could use the Internet's incredible resources, then it's one you can use again — and don't forget to share it with other teachers on the Net!

Sample Lesson Plans

It's one thing for a teacher to know how to navigate the Internet and find educational treasures — and quite another to incorporate it into classroom activities in a meaningful way.

Educators using the Internet crave hands-on, step-by-step methods for integrating the network into their curricula. That's what these lesson plans are for: to empower teachers to fulfill their educational objectives while learning to use the Internet and its resources. Many of these plans feature simple exercises that get teachers and students online.

How to Use These Plans

These lesson plans cover a variety of subjects and grade levels and have been arranged according to subject matter. Each plan includes objectives, materials, procedures, and addresses of Internet resources. The suggested grade levels are simply guidelines, and most of these plans can be modified for use in other grades. Some plans also feature extensions for advanced students. You can use these lessons and projects as they are, modify them to meet your needs, or augment them with Internet resources of your own.

Remember: the best lesson plans do not use the Internet as an end in itself. Rather, they employ it as a means to an end, incorporating its resources as an extra tool to attain a larger educational goal.

Autobiographical Writing   *Grade Levels: 3–12*

Students use the Internet to find grammar information, to write an autobiographical poem, and to email the poems to a partner class.

OBJECTIVES

- Practice writing with concrete and abstract nouns, adjectives, and adverbs.
- Write autobiographical poems to help students get to know each other.
- Communicate with and get to know a distant class via email.

MATERIALS

- Personal computer with an Internet connection
- Simple word processor and printer, or pencils and paper

PROCEDURE

1. Before beginning the project, find a class to communicate with via email. It can be a class you're doing other projects with or, to find a partner class, post queries to the appropriate education newsgroups or mailing lists.

2. Review the differences between concrete and abstract nouns, adjectives, and adverbs. Students can use the World Wide Web to access grammar tips and other usage documents at the University of Purdue Online Writing Lab (OWL).

   http://owl.english.purdue.edu/

3. Prepare your autobiographical poem in advance, and write it on a chalkboard or post it on a bulletin board in the classroom for students to read. Here's an example:

Line 1	Your first name	Vince
Line 2	Son or daughter of...	Vince and Georgette
Line 3	Four traits (adjectives)	curious, ambitious, funny, talkative
Line 4	Lover of (concrete nouns)	pizza, doughnuts, cats, bikes
Line 5	Who acts (adverbs)	cautiously
Line 6	Who needs (abstract nouns)	companionship
Line 7	Who fears (concrete nouns)	lightning
Line 8	Who hopes for (abstract nouns)	peace
Line 9	Resident of	Lancaster
Line 10	Your last name	DiStefano

Language Arts

4. Have students write their own autobiographical poems, then exchange them with a remote partner class via email. This is a great way to match students with similar interests for further correspondence.

EXTENSIONS

1. For a fun class period, distribute the students' poems randomly among the class. Have each student read the poem but omit the name. See if other students can guess the author.
2. Have each student use a computer illustration program to do a self-portrait. If the school has an image scanner, they can scan in a photo of themselves. Teach them how to attach graphics files to their email messages and send their drawings with the corresponding poems to their partner class.

Research Writing

Students research, write, and properly cite a report, using traditional and online resources for research.

OBJECTIVES

- Review the fundamentals of report or essay researching and writing.
- Write a report on a given topic.
- Practice locating information in the school library.
- Practice finding information on the Internet.
- Compare and contrast traditional research approaches with electronic information gathering.

MATERIALS

- Personal computer with an Internet connection
- Library resources, including magazines and newspapers, encyclopedias, and reference books

PROCEDURE

1. As a class, discuss the fundamentals of report writing, including selecting a topic, elements of a report (thesis, introduction, body, conclusion, bibliography), conducting library research (using card catalogs and reference materials), primary vs. secondary research, paraphrasing and copyright issues, methods for note-taking, and so forth. Students can tap into the following Internet resources for additional information.

    ### *University of Texas Writing Centers*
    http://www.en.utexas.edu
    http://uwc-server.fac.utexas.edu

    ### *Online Writer*
    http://www.missouri.edu/~writery/

    An accepted style for citing Internet resources is evolving. Discuss this issue with students. For background, try the site:
    http://www.connectedteacher.com/newsletter/citeintres.asp

2. Assign students a report on a topic of their choosing. The length of the report and the deadline depends on how much time you have for this project and students' current abilities. Give them some general categories, such as the environment, music, art, biology, law, health and medicine, government, or technology.

Language Arts

3. Have students conduct their research in the school library, in a city or county library, and on the Internet. Structure the assignment to allow ample time for students to select a topic, conduct preliminary research to narrow it down, further research their topics, write rough drafts, get teacher feedback, and revise the reports. Students should split their time equally between using traditional research methods and doing online research. Have them keep a log of the information they find via traditional sources and the information they find on the Internet, and how much time each method took.

4. Give students some starting points for conducting online topical research, but let them explore the Net on their own to track down the information they need. (Make sure they're under close supervision during their "explorations." They can work in pairs or in groups so they can police each other. Or have adult volunteers who can look over their shoulders as they wander online.) Students can use these Web sites to help them on their searches.

Alta Vista Home Page

http://www.altavista.digital.com

HotBot

http://www.hotbot.com

University of Purdue Research Starting Points

http://owl.english.purdue.edu/research.html

Yahoo!

http://www.yahoo.com

Students can use other online tools. For example, students writing papers on the future of virtual reality might want to look for information in the various computer newsgroups. Students could also join relevant mailing lists to send email queries to experts in the field.

5. After students have completed their papers, have the class discuss the differences between traditional research and online research. Which did they enjoy more? Which approach yielded the most information or the best information? Discuss the benefits and drawbacks of each approach. For example, most people have free access to libraries, but the information there might not be as up to date as that found online. Or a specific resource might be unavailable because it's being used by someone else. Also, doing research online allows you to search for information quickly from your workstation or download auxiliary materials such as graphics, but you need to have access to adequate computer equipment.

Fictional Character Resumé Grade Levels: 9–12

This lesson centers on job-searching and resumé creation for a character from fiction. Your students will choose new occupations for their literary figures to help their characters resolve the problems presented in the plot.

OBJECTIVES

- Read a short story.
- Identify the characterization and conflict(s) of a main character.
- Identify the sections and content of a resumé.
- Utilize literary elements of conflict, setting, and characterization to compile the details of a resumé.
- Create a resumé for a fictional character and find this character a new occupation that will improve his or her situation.

MATERIALS

- Computer with Internet access
- Local newspapers with employment listings
- Word processing software

PROCEDURES

1. Read one or more of the selections from the American Literature Survey site on the Internet: *Young Goodman Brown*, *Rip Van Winkle*, *Bartleby the Scrivener*, or *A Raisin in the Sun*. Or use current selections you've been reading in your Language Arts class as the literary backdrop for a fictional character resumé. Your students will become familiar with the process of writing a resumé and will choose new occupations for their characters that will help the characters resolve some of the problems presented in the plot. The more selections your class has read, the more characters your students can choose from. This activity will work with all pieces of literature that have a main character. Examples include Ahab from *Moby Dick*, Henry David Thoreau as himself in *Walden*, or the minister in *The Minister's Black Veil*.

   ### Rip Van Winkle

   http://www.cwrl.utexas.edu/~daniel/amlit/rvw/rvwtext.html

   ### Young Goodman Brown

   http://www.cwrl.utexas.edu/~daniel/amlit/goodman/goodmantext.html

Language Arts

Bartleby the Scrivener

http://www.cwrl.utexas.edu/~daniel/amlit/bartleby/bartleby.html

A Raisin in the Sun: synopsis

**http://www.cwrl.utexas.edu/~daniel/anderson/amlit/raisin/bmikosh/
act1scene1.html**

View the video excerpts from the film, *A Raisin in the Sun*, for clearer characterization.

"Eat Your Eggs..."

**http://www.cwrl.utexas.edu/~daniel/anderson/amlit/raisin/bmikosh/
RaisinHome.html**

2. Have your students collect all relevant characterization and conflict elements for their literary characters into a database. Your students must include as much description of the character's background and current status in the resumé as possible. What is the conflict this character is experiencing?

3. Distribute the employment sections of current local or national newspapers to your class. Tell your students to use the character data collected in step two to determine which advertised job would best aid the character's plight. For example (it can be humorous), Captain Ahab could retire as whaling ship captain and apply for a job as Cruise Director for Pacific Princess, and Bartleby could use a reduced-stress job far from Wall Street. See what solutions your students can find for these characters in the midst of turmoil and conflict.

4. Go to the Purdue Online Writing Lab's Resumé sites on the Internet for information on creating the format and content for a resumé.

Your Resumé

http://owl.english.purdue.edu/files/35.html

Resumé Sections

http://owl.english.purdue.edu/files/53.html

The Resumé: Making it Work for you
http://owl.english.purdue.edu/files/50.html

5. Have students create a resumé for their fictional character. Tell them to be as accurate as possible, using the story as the basis for what they write. To ensure a professional appearance, your students should create their resumés on a word processor. When they finish, your students should decide, on the basis of the job openings advertised in the newspaper's Help Wanted sections, where their characters should apply for jobs.

Language Arts

EXTENSIONS

1. Have your students dramatize what they can imagine happening in the job interviews of their fictional applicants. Students can work in small teams to generate interview questions based on job descriptions, previous experience, and other general "on-the-spot" interview questions that usually make us all nervous at one time or another. Urge your students to dress and act in accordance with their characters. Have the students playing the literary figures dress and speak from the setting of their story, while the students acting as the interviewers should dress and act "modern." Let your students perform their interviews for the class. Videotape their performances if possible.

2. Have your students create a resumé that they can imagine themselves using ten years in the future. Where do they think they will be then? Where will their life pursuits lead them? Be imaginative!

3. Have each of your students create real resumés they can use for applying for jobs now. Have your students look in the newspaper for job positions they can actually apply for.

Language Arts

Hamlet on Trial:
Innocent, Guilty, or Insane? Grade Levels: 9–12

Your students will gain a deeper understanding of *Hamlet* after putting Hamlet, the protagonist, on trial for the multiple murders in the play. This lesson is best introduced at the start of your Hamlet unit and implemented when your students complete their study of the play.

OBJECTIVES

- Read *Hamlet* by William Shakespeare.
- Use details, clues, examples from the text to formulate a case for or against Hamlet.
- Assume the roles of court figures.
- Engage in the trial of Hamlet.
- Deliberate a verdict and possible sentence based on the "facts" from the text.

MATERIALS

- Computer with Internet access
- Familiarity with roles in a court of law

PROCEDURES

1. Most of us have a difficult time understanding the complexities of a trial until we're part of the process, whether as defendant, plaintiff, or jury member. We might read about a crime and a conviction, but we rarely follow the steps in a trial. This lesson offers the opportunity to experience how a trial works.

    Your students have probably watched The People's Court or Court TV on cable. Some of them might have followed the sensationalized media coverage of the O. J. Simpson trial. Ask your students to share their feelings on the U.S. judicial system. Ask your students, through a show of hands, how many think that our justice system is effective or not, fair or not. Try to uncover as many angles and "not-thought-of" items in this process.

2. Tell your students to read *Hamlet* very carefully and to list character traits of Hamlet as they read. The entire play can take weeks of class time to read and discuss, so remind them daily to take the initiative to collect pertinent data. Perhaps a graded nightly journal entry would help your students stay on task.

Hamlet

http://the-tech.mit.edu/Shakespeare/Tragedy/hamlet/hamlet.html

3. Introduce the figures involved in a trial and the roles they serve, from the judge to the bailiff. Be sure all students get an active role. There are more than enough roles to fill! Make sure that your students understand their courtroom roles for this trial. Set a date for the trial well into the future so your students have enough time to research both their roles and the play. Remember, as in a court of law, only the facts are admissible. Determine if Hamlet is innocent, guilty, or insane, or any combination of these. Two trials never yield the same results. Remember, Shakespeare left no answers.

4. On the specified date, hold the trial. If possible, videotape the trial. Videotaping the student trial will be an invaluable resource for your future classes, as well as a great way for your current students to review their work.

EXTENSIONS

1. You can research the facts and hold trials for other Shakespearean tragic heroes. Consider, for example, Othello, Romeo, Macbeth, Julius Caesar, or Brutus. You can find all these plays, with helpful annotations, on the Internet.

   ### Julius Caesar

   http://the-tech.mit.edu/Shakespeare/Tragedy/juliuscaesar/juliuscaesar.html

   ### Romeo and Juliet

   http://the-tech.mit.edu/Shakespeare/Tragedy/romeoandjuliet/romeoandjuliet.html

   ### Othello

   http://the-tech.mit.edu/Shakespeare/Tragedy/othello/othello.html

   ### Macbeth

   http://the-tech.mit.edu/Shakesp7re/Tragedy/macbeth/macbeth.html

2. Compare and contrast the O.J. Simpson trial to Othello. Your students can get a fresh perspective on the play and on the Simpson trial by linking these two figures together. Discuss the themes and situations with your students and have them compose an essay exploring the similarities and differences.

   ### Othello

   http://the-tech.mit.edu/Shakespeare/Tragedy/othello/othello.html

3. While your class is in a deliberative mode, why not put William Shakespeare on trial? There has been a long standing debate on who actually wrote the plays: a Stratford resident named William Shakespeare or an Oxford earl. Send your students to the library to research both sides of the argument and make their own decisions. The more familiar your students become with the works, life, and times of William Shakespeare and Elizabethan England, the more they'll be able to support their conclusions.

Language Arts

Mathematics _Lesson Plans_

A Million and Counting   _Grade Levels: 6–9_

In this lesson, your students will discover how math and remote sensing were used to solve a problem. They will use the same techniques to solve a similar problem based in their hometown.

OBJECTIVES

- Express mathematical concepts in writing.
- Solve problems by using a formula for area.
- Use mapping skills to solve problems.

MATERIALS

- Calculators
- Compasses
- Local maps with the school's location pinpointed

PROCEDURES

1. Questions often arise about the size of the crowd attending an enormous outdoor event. Event organizers, the media, and law enforcement agencies offer estimates, but when masses of people attend an event, no one is really sure whose count is the closest to being accurate. At the Million Man March held in the fall of 1995 in Washington, D.C., many people wondered whether the much-publicized goal of having one million men attend was reached. The National Park Service estimated the crowd size to be about 400,000 people, while the event's organizers claimed a million people were present. Dr. Farouk El-Baz, a scientist from Boston University, decided to solve this dilemma by using mathematics and remote sensing. Thanks to satellite aerial photos and computers, Dr. El-Baz set out to count the people. He used the basic geometric principle for area to solve this problem.

2. Send your students to the Million Man March Web pages at the Observatorium. Have your students research the methods used to solve this problem. After they look through this site, instruct your students to write a one-page essay describing how this scientist used area to solve this problem.

Observatorium

http://observe.ivv.nasa.gov/observe.html

Million Man March

http://observe.ivv.nasa.gov/nasa/education/exhibits/march/march_0.html

3. One method Dr. El-Baz used was to find the maximum number of people standing in one square meter. Conduct this study with your class. Have two students mark a square in a corner of the classroom with each side measuring one meter. Send your students, one at a time, to the square until the square is filled to the maximum. How many students can stand inside the square? Tell them they will use this number in their calculations. Give each student a local map with your school's location pinpointed. Ideally, the map will have at least 600 square meters on each side of the school.

4. Now give your students their maps and their own problem to solve. Tell them a student rally is scheduled at your school, and 878,589 people (the same number of people Dr. El-Baz counted at the Million Man March) are coming. Have your students calculate the size of the area this student rally will cover. The catch is that, moving from the center, the size of the crowd thins out in concentric circles, and the radius of each succeeding circle increases by 50 meters. Every 50 meters away from the center, the concentration diminishes by 2 students per square meter. Tell your students that they are to find the area covered by students at this rally and draw the circle that represents this area on their local map. They should also draw and label the concentric circles of concentration on the map.

EXTENSIONS

1. Show your students how remote sensing was used to solve another problem. Satellite photography was used to track the rain forest depletion in South America. Take your students on a tour through this Web site at the Observatorium. You can assign them to research beyond this for extra credit.

Rain Forest Sensing

http://observe.ivv.nasa.gov/nasa/education/exhibits/history/history_8.html

2. For Black History Month in February, you can combine this math lesson that uses the Million Man March with a discussion about contemporary African-American authors. You'll find information about the American writer Alice Walker included and her award-winning novel, *The Color Purple*, at the Web site below.

Alice Walker

http://www.cwrl.utexas.edu/~mmaynard/Walker/walker.htm

3. Have your students create their own problems that can be solved using remote sensing and mathematics. They might, for instance, try to find the size of an oil spill in an ocean, the amount of traffic congestion, or how much smog hovers over a large city.

Mathematics

Economics: The Stock Market

Students are required to pick stocks, track their progress via the Internet, and try an online stock market simulation.

OBJECTIVES

- Understand how the stock market works and what factors affect it.
- Participate in simulated market transactions and track progress of investments.

MATERIALS

- Personal computer with an Internet connection
- Word processor and printer

PROCEDURE

1. Provide an overview of how the stock market works. Explain the traditional methods of tracking stock activity, such as newspapers and brokerage services.

2. Have each student pick one to five stocks to monitor for several weeks. Each student should keep a log of their stocks' activities. Use these Internet resources to access up-to-date stock market information and news that could affect their holdings.

   ### StockMaster

   http://www.stockmaster.com

   ### Quote.com

   http://www.quote.com

3. Using the same selected stocks, have students try out an online, interactive stock market simulation via the PAWWS Portfolio Management Challenge, a free financial service on the World Wide Web. Or use stock market simulations found in most commercial online services. Students will buy, sell, and value their portfolios for a specified period of time. Students should carefully read the rules and instructions first. Each student should print out stock information and keep it in a binder.

   ### PAWWS Portfolio Management Challenge

   http://pawws.secapl.com/G_phtml/top.html

   Click on Portfolio Management Challenge for an overview, then jump back to play the simulation. Teachers may want to review these materials first.

4. At the end of the simulation, the class should examine each student's results and announce the "Financial Wizard" award winner.

EXTENSIONS

1. Invite a local stockbroker or financial analyst, preferably one knowledgeable about financial resources on the Internet, to speak to the class. Compose a list of questions to ask in class or send a list to the volunteer before the visit.

Mathematics

Geometric Probability

Let your students explore the Internet and have fun with plane figures in geometry. For this lesson, your students explore simple probability and express probability geometrically.

OBJECTIVES

- Represent simple probability geometrically using the area of plane figures.
- Count a random sample to determine the probability of an event occurring.
- Calculate simple probability.
- Work effectively in groups.

MATERIALS

- Computer with Internet access
- Graph paper
- Map or globe of the world

PROCEDURES

1. Draw a circle on the board. Ask what uses a circle has in real life. Get as many responses as you can. Now draw a square or a triangle on the board and ask the same question. Any use for these polygons they can think up is great. Tell your students that they will be using these and other shapes to represent probability. They will be using drawings to represent numbers and chance. To do this they will need to remember their previous work with fractions.

2. First have your students go through a simple exercise where they will be finding fractional parts of polygons. For example, give them a couple of minutes to find the fractional area that is:

    a. 1/3 of a given circle
    b. 1/4 of a given square
    c. 1/6 of a given triangle

3. In this lesson, your students will be using challenge problems from Math Magic. Tell them to go to Level 7-9, Cycle 1 under the menu Past Challenges and read the introduction to probability.

    ### Math Magic, Level 7-9, Cycle 1

    ftp://forum.swarthmore.edu/mathmagic/7-9/cycle.001

    Your students should work through the exercises in Cycle 1. They will be determining probability based on the fractional areas in the figure compared to the total area.

4. Have your students apply this probability model to the workings of DNA. Ask them to go to the Exploratorium Web site for background information on the DNA structure of mutating fruit flies for a good example of chance and probability in the real world.

    ### The Exploratorium

    http://www.exploratorium.edu/learning_studio/lsxhibit.html

    ### Mutant Fruit Flies

    http://www.exploratorium.edu/exhibits/mutant_flies/mutant_flies.html

5. Have your students find the probability of each mutant type of fruit fly from the DNA structure. There are only four different chromosomes, so there would be a small amount of combinations. On their graph paper, have your students represent each mutant case as a fractional area of a plane figure. You may need to clarify how to start finding the combinations of flies for the students.
6. Walk around the class while they are working and ask the students to explain what they are doing and how they will be attempting it on paper.

EXTENSIONS

1. Have your students break into groups of four. Give each group a bag of M&M's and graph paper. Each group will be responsible for counting the number of M&M's in each color and the total number of M&M's. From these numbers, your students can calculate the probability of drawing a certain color out of the bag of candy. This calculation is done for each color. Using the graph paper, your students now must draw a diagram that represents the probabilities of each color by area. The areas must be color coded. The area of each section must be equal to a fraction of the total area; that is its probability. At the end of the activity, let your students eat the M&M's.
2. Have your students experiment with a deck of cards instead of candy. Have them represent different hands in geometric areas. For this extension, you can use Math Magic Level #10-12, Cycle 16. This site poses an extra question of a replacement or non-replacement event.

    ### Math Magic Level 10-12, Cycle 16

    ftp://forum.swarthmore.edu/mathmagic/10-12/cycle.016

Mathematics

The Metric Sport

Grade Levels: 7–9

In this lesson, your students will discover the basics of the metric system and apply this knowledge to the sport of track and field. Let your students discover conversion basics on the Internet.

OBJECTIVES

- Students will learn about the metric system.
- Students will convert using different prefixes.
- Students will solve problems involving the metric system.

MATERIALS

- Computer with Internet access

PROCEDURES

1. Despite efforts to incorporate the metric system, U.S. students are most familiar with the English system of measurement. Learning the metric system is important because of its widespread use in the scientific community and the rest of the world. Begin this lesson by giving your students a background into the prefixes derived from the metric system. These prefixes are classic references to the numbers they represent. Write a few of the prefixes on the board. Have your students write some words they already know using these prefixes. They need not be words from the metric system. Some good prefixes to use are kilo, milli, centi, or deca, and offer words like "century," "decagon," or "millipede" as examples of the words from the metric system. Of course, not all words with the prefixes have a metric meaning, for example, the word "million."

2. Send your students to the Metric System page at the Basic Math Concepts and Fundamentals site on the Internet. Have them read all the prefixes and discover their metric meanings.

Metric System and Unit Conversion
http://edie.cprost.sfu.ca/~rhlogan/metric.html

Basic Math Concepts and Fundamentals
http://edie.cprost.sfu.ca/~rhlogan/basicmth.html

3. Now have your students convert within the metric system using the prefixes mentioned above. Use the *Metric System* lesson of the *Basic Math* page to show your students the methods of converting. I suggest they use the decimal equivalent system to convert, but if you have a tried method, please use it. By using the chart with the decimal equivalents, your students can convert any number in two simple steps: 1) convert it to the basic unit; and 2) convert it to the needed unit by using the appropriate decimal equivalent.

Mathematics

4. For a real-world application, have your students consider the sport of track and field. Have your students solve the following problem using their metric skills:

    Carla just completed a decathlon, but the judge measured all the events using the wrong units. Have your students convert the measurements to the correct units and see how well Carla performed. Here are Carla's results as reported by the judge:

    Discus 4,085 cm, Pole Vault 508 cm, Shotput 1,410 cm, High Jump 2,090 mm, 100,000 mm run 11"02 seconds, Javelin 49,520 mm, 40,000 cm run 50"17 seconds, 1,500,000 cm run 4'34"31 seconds, Long Jump 742 cm, 110,000 mm hurdles 13"59 seconds.

    Fill the chart below and compare Carla's results with the current leader's.

Events	Carla	Leader
100 m run	?	11"02 seconds
Long Jump	?	7.34 meters
Shotput	?	14.20 meters
High Jump	?	2.10 meters
400 m run	?	49"17 seconds
110 m hurdles	?	14"49 seconds
Discus	?	40.56 meters
Pole Vault	?	5.10 meters
Javelin	?	49.48 meters
1,500 m run	?	4'44"41 seconds

5. On a piece of paper instruct your students to summarize the basics of converting in the metric system. This description should be at least one paragraph long and written in complete sentences.

EXTENSIONS

1. Choose some objects, such a pencil, a sheet of paper, or book, without measurements marked on them. Have your students decide which units would be best to measure these objects. Challenge them to find not only the basic unit but the correct prefix to make significant measurements.

2. Instruct your students to take the Online Metric Quiz on the Internet. This quiz will test your students' skills in knowing the prefixes and being able to convert between measurements. Also students will use the metric system for measuring all types of quantities, such as weight, volume, and area.

Metric System

http://edie.cprost.sfu.ca/~rhlogan/metric.html

Mathematics

Science *Lesson Plans*

Crowns of Gold

Grade Levels: 7–9

Students will solve a classic problem from antiquity using both their knowledge of density and their measuring skills.

OBJECTIVES

- Measure mass and volume of objects.
- Calculate density.
- Solve problems using experimental methods.

MATERIALS

- Computer with Internet access

PROCEDURES

1. One of our most useful measurable quantities of matter is density. We rely on density to keep us buoyant in water or to send cameras to the bottom of the ocean. Your students will recreate an ancient experiment from the time of Archimedes, with a twist.

2. Have your students go to The Golden Crown page on the Archimedes Home Page. Ask them to read the story about Archimedes and his task to find whether a crown was entirely made of gold. Now your students are to take on a similar challenge. Tell them they have been given ten crowns, and they must determine which one is pure gold. Send them to the density module at the IPPEX Science Education site and perform this tutorial.

   ### Archimedes Home Page
   http://www.mcs.drexel.edu/~crorres/Archimedes/contents.html

   ### The Golden Crown
   http://www.mcs.drexel.edu/~crorres/Archimedes/Crown/CrownIntro.html

   ### IPPEX Science Education
   http://ippex.pppl.gov/ippex/

   ### Density Module
   http://ippex.pppl.gov/ippex/module_3/density.html

Science

3. Your students may now proceed to the Density Lab to perform their experiments. Ten "hunks" of material are provided, one for each crown. Using the instruments given, your students are to find which one is gold. Have your students complete the following chart with the data they collect. They are not to calculate densities until they have taken all of their measurements.

Density Lab

http://ippex.pppl.gov/ippex/module_3/densitylab.html

Description	Mass (g)	Volume (ml)	Float (Y/N)	Density
1.				
2.				
3.				
4.				
5.				
6.				
7.				
8.				
9.				
10.				

4. After finding the densities for each hunk, your students should go to the following page on the site to determine the material for each hunk.

Common Densities

http://ippex.pppl.gov/ippex/module_3/commondensity.html

EXTENSIONS

1. Go further to study the fourth state of matter called plasma. Compare plasma to the other states of matter.

States of Matter

http://ippex.pppl.gov/ippex/About_fusion/fusion_doc3.html

2. You cannot forget volume. Follow along with Archimedes and his study of solids. Let your students find the volume of these Archimedean solids.

Archimedean Solids

http://www.mcs.drexel.edu/~crorres/Archimedes/Solids/Pappus.html

Science

Plant Anatomy

Students are required to work in teams, conduct research with printed and Internet resources, write figuratively, and use illustration software.

OBJECTIVES

- Use the Internet to find information about plant anatomy.
- Think creatively to find analogies between plant parts and everyday objects or activities.
- Work cooperatively with other students in teams.

MATERIALS

- Personal computer with an Internet connection
- Word processor
- Graphics-capable printer

PROCEDURE

1. Students must define "analogy" and come up with several of their own analogies for the next class.
2. Divide the class into teams of three students. List the following plant parts (and more, if desired) on a bulletin or chalk board.

roots	vascular cambium
flowers	casparian strip
stems	latent bud
phloem	leaves
seeds	xylem

3. Explain that the purpose of the project is to write analogies for these plant parts. Here's an example: Leaves of green plants are analogous to factory assembly lines. The epidermis is like the outer wall; palisade cells are like assembly lines; chloroplasts are like workers moving from place to place along those assembly lines, using energy (carbon dioxide and water) to bring together raw materials to produce a finished product, glucose. Glucose is then transferred via a conveyor belt, the phloem, to the warehouse, or root. And as in real factories (unless there are second or third shifts), production stops at night.

   Each team selects one plant part and finds as much information as it can using texts, library materials, and Internet resources. Allow sufficient time for teams to gather enough materials to use to create their analogies. For information on plant anatomy, students can access these World Wide Web sites.

Dictionary of Cell Biology

http://www.mblab.gla.ac.uk/~julian/Dict.html

Biodiversity and Biological Collections

http://muse.bio.cornell.edu

4. After they've gathered enough information, have the teams brainstorm and write their analogies. Teams should preferably bring their research to class and compose the analogy together on word processors (see extension). Each analogy should be no more than one page. For help with using figurative language, students can access the World Wide Web.

Networked Writing Environment

http://www.ucet.ufl.edu/writing/nwe.html

Purdue University Online Writing Lab (OWL)

http://owl.english.purdue.edu

5. Have the teams illustrate and label the plant part and its analogous counterpart. Make copies of each group's text and illustrations and distribute to the class.

EXTENSION

Access these Bionet newsgroups and post the text of the students' analogies. Invite readers to respond with feedback or to contribute their own analogies. If students have trouble composing their analogies, they can post requests for assistance here.

news:sci.bio.botany	biology and related sciences
news:bionet.cellbiol	general discussions about cell biology
news:bionet.plants	discussions about all aspects of plant biology

Science

The Solar Travel Agent

Grade Levels: 8–12

Your students use their imagination and creativity to research, write, and produce travel brochures for the sun and the nine planets.

OBJECTIVES

- Research a specific topic using various resources.
- Present information in a persuasive context.
- Produce a simple form of media.
- Work effectively as a team.

MATERIALS

- Computer with Internet access
- Travel brochures, one for each student, to a wide variety of destinations. The more exotic and far away the better!
- Desktop publishing program or your school's print shop
- Large sheets of paper
- Printer

PROCEDURES

1. To reach potential customers, many businesses spend a lot of time and money developing print material, such as brochures, to explain and sell their goods and services. Airlines, tourist offices, and travel agencies, for example, produce and distribute brochures extolling the virtues of beautiful destinations. Tell your students these businesses know these brochures do a good job persuading customers to visit the places featured.

   Now hand out your travel brochures. Ask your students if looking at these brochures makes them want to go on a trip. Ask them what about the brochures makes these places sound so appealing. Is it the brochure copy? The pictures? Both? Do these brochures have a way of making them feel excited about traveling to these places? Can they imagine themselves feeling happy on vacation at these places? If so, these travel brochures have done their job. Now tell your students they will be creating travel brochures for even more exotic, faraway places. They will be creating travel brochures for the nine planets and the sun.

2. Divide your class into ten groups, one group for each planet and one group for the sun. Each group will write, design, and produce a travel brochure for a different solar body.

3. Your students' first task is to research their solar body. Explain that their brochures should offer the same kind of information found in the travel brochures they've read. For example, their brochures should cover accommodations, restaurants, recreational activities, sites to tour, weather conditions, travel and dress requirements, and indigenous life forms. You can include other categories of your choice. Send them to

the Views of the Solar System site on the Web and to the library to gather information. Not all the information on their brochures has to be factual. They'll use their imaginations and have some fun as they write the copy for, let's say, mountain bike trails on the moon or music clubs on Venus.

Views of the Solar System

http://www.hawastsoc.org/solar/homepage.htm

4. Have each student group write a rough draft of their brochure and plan its layout on a large sheet of paper. Remind them they're using pictures, graphics, and prose to "sell" their planet. Some of the images they can download from the Web. They can also create their own art with the desktop publisher or they can use clip art that you supply.

5. After you okay the rough drafts and layouts, your student groups can work together to produce their final products. The groups can produce their brochures using a desktop publishing program or the school's print shop.

6. Display the brochures around your classroom or school. Don't be surprised if people want to sign up for these fanciful trips.

EXTENSIONS

1. Take this lesson a step further with a role-playing exercise in persuasion. Have your students be salespeople for the trip they have constructed. If they wish, let them dress as if they're presenting their travel ideas to a social club looking for a trip to take together. Instruct your students to write the five-minute speech highlighting the fun and excitement of such a trip. They should include details such as the fuzzy glow of Venus's atmosphere or the way light explodes off of Neptune's glacial flows.

2. Tie math into this lesson by having your class create a pricing guide for these jaunts in the solar system. Calculate how much it costs to fly to each planet. Designate the cost by mile or light year. Go to Views of the Solar System to find the average distances to each planet.

Views of the Solar System

http://www.hawastsoc.org/solar/homepage.htm

3. Your students can become space traffic controllers as they compare and contrast space travel distances. Using the planetary distances found on the Views of the Solar System, have your students create flight schedules using the time necessary to travel to and from Pluto, the farthest planet, as the time frame. For example, your students will discover they could make nearly eight round trips to Venus in the same amount of time required to make a one-way trip from Earth to Jupiter.

Views of the Solar System

http://www.hawastsoc.org/solar/homepage.htm

Science

Where's the Beefalo?

Grade Levels: 9–10

In this lesson students will be exploring the science of producing beefalo from cow and buffalo cattle strains.

OBJECTIVES

- Students will discover the benefits of selective breeding.
- Students will create a model of selective breeding.
- Students will solve problems using multiplication of fractions.

MATERIALS

- Computer with Internet access
- Paper and writing materials

PROCEDURES

1. Selective breeding in the livestock industry has produced many advances for better and more efficient livestock breeds. One the best advances was the discovery of the beefalo. Beefalo are a cross between buffalo and beef cattle. They are 3/8 buffalo and 5/8 bovine. This mix renders the best traits from both strains.
2. Your students each start with 10 beef cattle and 10 buffalo. They are to produce grandchildren that are beefalo from these two herds using a family tree. They must produce hybrids that are exactly a 3/8 to 5/8 mix of beef cattle to buffalo.
3. Instruct your students to go to the Breeds of Livestock site to get more information on the Beefalo. They should specifically find the hybrid ratio on their own and some history of the beefalo.

Breeds of Livestock

http://www.ansi.okstate.edu/breeds/

Beefalo Cattle

http://www.ansi.okstate.edu/breeds/cattle/beefalo/

4. Instruct your students to make a generation tree for the breeding of the beefalo. They are to use their knowledge of multiplication of fractions to calculate the breeding that must occur. You may choose to have a ready-made example to give them an idea of what you want.
5. Now have your students organize their herds so that they can produce the most beefalo in two generations. Make it a contest. Challenge your students to find the highest number of the combinations of cattle.

EXTENSIONS

1. A fascinating topic to cover with your students is genealogy. Just about everybody in the United States is from somewhere else. You can give your students some perspective on this at the American Immigration Home Page. They will love to deduce where some of their traits may have come from. Take them back two or three generations. You could focus on personalities or physical traits.

    ### American Immigration Home Page

    http://www.bergen.org/AAST/Projects/Immigration/

2. Another spin on this lesson would be a math lesson. Use combinations or permutations to find the maximum number of offspring that could be generated from the given herds. This can become challenging when your students calculate the results over two generations.

Social Studies *Lesson Plans*

Women's Studies   *Grade Levels: 6–12*

Students use the Internet to research women's issues and examine historical, constitutional, biographical, and current material, and then to write a paper.

OBJECTIVES

- Gather information about the women's suffrage movement and other historical, gender-related constitutional issues.
- Find biographical information about important women in American history.
- Keep up to date with current women's issues.

MATERIALS

- Personal computer with an Internet connection
- Word processor and printer

PROCEDURE

1. Midway through your study of women's issues or the suffrage movement, have students go online to access an electronic version of the U.S. Constitution. Review critical amendments and sections pertaining to women's rights.

   #### Cornell Law School
   http://www.law.cornell.edu/constitution/constitution.overview.html

2. Then, students should look for two kinds of information: historical information about notable women and the suffrage movement as well as classic texts dealing with gender issues such as rights to property; and information about current women's issues, such as the glass ceiling. Here are some starting points.

   #### InforMN's Women's Studies Database
   http://www.inform.umd.edu/EdRes/Topic/WomensStudies/

   #### The University of Wisconsin System Women's Studies Librarian
   http://www.library.wisc.edu/libraries/WomensStudies/

Social Studies

3. Students should pick a topic based on their Internet research and their interests for a brief reaction paper. Topics can range from "The Poetry of Important Women in American History," "What would Elizabeth Cady Stanton be doing today?" or "Women in Today's Congress." Students can use the school library to find information unavailable online.

4. Students should check to see if their topics are being addressed through current legislation about gender issues. They can search these sites.

Thomas Web

http://thomas.loc.gov

Congress.Org

http://congress.org

EXTENSIONS

1. Students who want to become more involved in women's issues can access the WomensNet Web site. They'll find contact information for dozens of national and international organizations. Give extra credit to students who write to and receive information from groups that interest them.
http://www.igc.apc.org/womensnet/

2. Have students write letters or send email to members of Congress and the president about women's issues important to them. For postal and email addresses for members of Congress, return to the Thomas Web site, or try these sites.
mailto:president@whitehouse.gov

Social Studies

Geography

Students are expected to use the Internet to do research and to use a variety of tools to write and illustrate a book.

OBJECTIVES

- Create an A–Z illustrated handbook about a specific state using a computer.

MATERIALS

- Personal computer with an Internet connection
- Word processor and simple illustration or layout software
- Graphics-capable printer
- Paper, markers, and other art supplies

PROCEDURE

1. Students will each make a book about a state of their choosing and pretend their books are to educate students visiting the United States for the first time. Each page of a student's book will present a letter of the alphabet and a fact that begins with that letter. The fact can be several paragraphs, a picture, or an illustration on a topic relevant to that state. For example, the "A" page for Florida might have a student's drawing of alligators; the "A" page for Pennsylvania might have a picture of an Amish buggy; and the "A" page for Ohio might include a list of facts about Akron. Students can include whatever they want, but they must explain how it is relevant to their state.
2. Have students use the Internet and the school library to find information about their state. Be flexible about how they create their books - students can draw pictures or use photographs taken on a vacation. Challenge them to be creative. These resources can help.

city.net
http://www.city.net

USA CityLink
http://usacitylink.com

The 50 States and Capitals
http://www.scvol.com:80/States/

Yahoo! — Regional:U.S. States
http://www.yahoo.com/Regional/U_S__States/

3. Instruct students to employ a variety of tools to complete their books, such as word processors, desktop publishing software, graphics downloaded from the Internet, or art supplies.
4. Give each student a folder or binder for his or her work. Set aside class time so students can exchange books before taking them home.

EXTENSIONS

1. As a class, discuss the various entries for each student's book. Which pages could only belong to a certain state? Could any pages fit into almost any state's book?
2. Share students' work with partner classes overseas who want to learn more about the states.

Social Studies

American &
Soviet Governments

Grade Levels: 7–12

Students are required to download materials from the Internet, discuss the style and rhetoric of political writings, use a word processor, search the Internet via keywords, and write a paper about Russia and the former U.S.S.R.

OBJECTIVES

- Learn the differences between the values in the Communist Manifesto and the Declaration of Independence, and how these documents were regarded by Russia and the United States during the Cold War years.
- Compare and contrast the tone and language of the U.S. and Soviet government documents.
- Explore the Soviet Archives Exhibit to learn how Communist theory translated into everyday Soviet life.
- Write a paper about one subject in Russian history or culture.

MATERIALS

- Personal computer with Internet access
- Word processor

PROCEDURE

1. Provide a brief overview of the events leading to the development of Communism and then the Cold War. Students should be familiar with the Declaration of Independence and the evolution of the U.S. Constitution.

2. Find and download the complete text of the Communist Manifesto by going to this location.

   Young Communist League: Manifesto of the Communist Party

   http://www.yclusa.org/readup/manread.html

   Have students examine the dictionary meaning of *manifesto*. Identify language in the document that qualifies the work as such and have students find key points and phrases from the document. As a class, discuss the tone, language, and euphemisms in the writing. Provide them with keywords such as "liberty," "property," "rights," and "labor." Instruct them to use the word processor's "search" or "find" function to jump to noteworthy sections.

3. Use the World Wide Web to visit the first floor of the Library of Congress' Soviet Archives to see how ideas in the Manifesto translated into everyday life. For example, discuss how the language and ideas found in the Manifesto led to living conditions not necessarily envisioned by its authors.

   http://sunsite.unc.edu/expo/soviet.exhibit/soviet.archive.html

   Have students discuss how the ideas expressed in the Constitution and the Declaration of Independence are translated in everyday life in the United States. Have students give examples for both countries.

Social Studies

4. Visit the second floor of the exhibit to read about Soviet-American relations during the Cold War.

5. Create a list of possible essay or term paper subjects. Have each student or small teams of students choose one. Topics could include the lives of Marx or Engels, living conditions under Stalin, Russian culture, the Soviet-U.S. nuclear arms race, the economic consequences of communism, the attempted coup of 1991, or any topic covered in the Soviet Archives.

6. Have students use the Internet to research their topics. A good place to start is this home page on the Web.

Yahoo!

http://www.yahoo.com

Scroll to the bottom to find the search interface. Enter a keyword, click on the World Wide Web and Gopher buttons, and select a maximum number of hits (resources found on the Internet) to return. Students may need to practice selecting keywords until they find enough leads for research.

Here are more Internet sites about Russia.

Window to Russia

http://www.wtr.ru/

St. Petersburg Web

http://www.spb.su

Dazhdbog's Grandchildren (Russian culture and heritage)

http://metalab.unc.edu/sergei/Grandsons.html

Novgorod on the Web

http://www.novsu.ac.ru/novgorod/novgorod.html

Civil War Time Line

Grade Levels: 6–9

This lesson gives students an opportunity to bring the events of the Civil War to life in a "virtual" history project.

MATERIALS

- Computer with Internet access
- Large classroom area
- Maps of the United States
- Props as determined by student groups

OBJECTIVES

- Research Civil War information from time line
- Work effectively in groups
- Visualize and "physicalize" Civil War events
- Present virtual project to class

PROCEDURES

1. Ask your students if they've ever seen a war room in a movie, or if they've ever played a game of chess. Both are examples of "physicalizing" a battle, whether it's a competitive board game between friends or a depiction of a full-scale war between countries. Both offer excellent ways to show your students, who often have a difficult time visualizing events from text and maps alone, troop movement, strategic locations, and changes in command. Tell your class they will create similar representations to show the events of the Civil War.

2. Divide your class into five large groups. Each group will represent one of the five years of the Civil War: 1861, 1862, 1863, 1864, and 1865. Go to the Civil War Time Line on the Internet and have each group read the three pages of brief text outlining the major events of each year. All the events from each year are linked to each other and to the outcome of the war in a step-by-step fashion. Your students should read the summaries and view the photos from each selection to understand the significant events of the entire war before they begin concentrating on their particular year. While they are reading, tell your students to think of ways to take the information from their computer screens to the classroom in a virtual presentation. Each group must devise a way to depict the events. For example, students could create a war room, play a game of human chess, or use a Lite-Brite game used to show troop movements in a battle. Urge them to think of creative ways to bring the past alive. Then tell the student groups to concentrate on gathering and arranging the information about their group's year.

Social Studies

Civil War Time Line (All groups)

http://rs6.loc.gov/ammem/tl1861.html

1861 Events and Photographs (Group 1)

http://rs6.loc.gov/ammem/tl1861.html

1862 Events and Photographs (Group 2)

http://rs6.loc.gov/ammem/tl1862.html

1863 Events and Photographs (Group 3)

http://rs6.loc.gov/ammem/tl1863.html

1864 Events and Photographs (Group 4)

http://rs6.loc.gov/ammem/tl1864.html

1865 Events and Photographs (Group 5)

http://rs6.loc.gov/ammem/tl1865.html

Now have all your students look at the following site for more information and background on Civil War events.

Other Photographs (All groups)

http://rs6.loc.gov/ammem/cwphome.html

Camp Life (All groups)

http://www.cr.nps.gov/csd/gettex/

3. Have each group present their virtual program to the class. Allow a class period per group so each group has ample time for setting up props, providing background information, and answering questions. Each group should be prepared to discuss why they chose to present their material the way they did and how they arranged the information and selected their props. Remind your students that they can use the entire room, including desks, chairs, and other students. Encourage them to think of any items they may need to bring into school as props. If possible, videotape the presentations. You can add the videotape to your multimedia collection as a reference for future presentations, as well as offer it to your students to view and critique their own presentations.

4. Have each student group create a quiz using the material they presented for their year. After you approve the quiz for fairness and appropriateness, have the group give the quiz to the rest of the class.

Social Studies

EXTENSIONS

1. Have your class research the food available to Civil War soldiers, which was often quite meager. Your class could make johnnycakes, corn bread, or grits. You could also open cans of beans and dried corn, and fry slabs of the worst-looking bacon you can find to simulate the quality of meat most soldiers ate. By today's standards, soldiers on both sides of the conflict ate very poorly.

2. Have a Civil War reenactment authority come to your class in costume to do a presentation and to answer questions about this popular hobby. Y

3. When all presentations have been given, allow your student groups to create "what if" scenarios based on their understanding of the events in the Civil War. For example, what if Fort Sumter had not been taken? How might the entire war have changed?

Social Studies

Join an Internet Project

Once you get comfortable with adding Net components to your lesson plans, you'll want to begin integrating Internet projects into your curriculum. These projects require students to use the Internet's navigation and communication tools to get involved in data exchanges, team writing projects, vicarious world explorations, and even global grocery shopping.

Dozens of mailing lists and the Usenet newsgroups are full of "requests for participation" in hundreds of Internet projects. Some projects are big affairs and are run by multimillion-dollar publishing companies such as MECC and Scholastic. But a greater number of them are smaller, teacher-created projects. Both provide equally powerful and valuable learning experiences for your students.

Types of Projects

There are five different types of Internet projects you can join. Depending upon the grade level you teach and subject matter you specialize in, several types of projects may be more suited to your needs.

- **Online Correspondence and Exchanges:** Involves setting up keypal (email penpal) connections between your students, their online peers, and subject matter experts (SMEs) such as scientists and engineers working in the field. This also includes the formation of learning circles.
- **Information Gathering:** These projects challenge students to use the Internet to collect, analyze, compare, and reflect upon different sources of information.
- **Problem Solving and Competitions:** Online competitions are projects through which students must use the Internet and other sources to solve problems while competing with other classrooms.
- **WebQuests:** A WebQuest is a learning activity in which students explore and collect a body of online information and make sense of it — usually by creating Web pages as the outcome. It's also the newest type of Internet project that's making a big impact in wired K-12 schools.
- **Online Conferencing:** Requires students to use online chat rooms or audio or video conferencing software to complete various project objectives.

Without the Internet, these classroom projects would be limited to use inside a single school. With Internet access, educators and students can take full advantage of these project models to link up remote classrooms located in nearly 200 countries worldwide to exchange information, collaborate, and solve common problems.

Where to Find Projects

Before you begin creating your own Internet projects, it's suggested that you join at least two ongoing Internet projects. By participating, you'll learn about how a project can and should run, and you'll generate ideas for your first self-created project. Following are some of the main places to visit to keep up-to-date with the latest projects that you and your students can join.

Global SchoolNet Foundation

http://www.gsn.org

HILITES

http://archives.gsn.org/hilites/

IECC-Projects

http://www.stolaf.edu/network/iecc/iecc-projects.html

Houghton Mifflin Project Center

http://www.hmco.com/hmco/school/projects/index.html

How to Plan Your Own Project

Once your students have participated in an online project, it will be easy to see how such projects generate student excitement and expand learning potential.

While you can participate in projects run by organizations or other teachers, creating *your own* project is the best way to stretch your Internet skills and meet your educational goals using this new technology.

Follow these eight steps — many based on guidelines by the Global SchoolNet Foundation — for creating a successful Internet project.

Eight Steps to a Successful Project

1. Think about your curriculum goals. What content do you want to help your students master, and can a telecommunications project be used as a resource? List the skills you want to teach or enrich your class, such as critical thinking, writing, or teamwork.
2. Go online to see how other teachers are structuring their projects. Good starting points include the Global SchoolNet Foundation and IECC Projects database.
3. Once you've become familiar with online projects, revisit your curriculum and teaching goals to come up with the type, topic, and content for your project.
4. Design your project with specific goals, tasks, and outcomes. The more specific you are, the better; and the more closely aligned with traditional instructional objectives, the better.
5. Set specific beginning and ending dates for your project, and set precise deadlines for participant responses. Make a time line of important deadlines and dates. Give plenty of lead time between your announcement of the project and its launch.
6. Use the template that follows to design a call for participation in your project. Be sure it includes examples of the kinds of writing or data students are expected to submit. Also be sure to give your readers clear guidelines and expectations regarding your project. Teachers should be able to tell at a glance whether or not they wish to participate in your project.

"Call for Participation" Template

- **A Call for Collaboration.** Please print and distribute this to teachers you know who may be interested in participating.
- **Project.** Name of your project.
- **Date.** Give the start and end dates of the project. Leave at least five weeks before the start of the project to permit enough people to respond to your call for collaboration.
- **Purpose.** Give a brief, two- to three-sentence summary of the purpose of your project. What will students learn?
- **Subjects.** In one or two sentences, state the curriculum areas that will be addressed by this project.
- **Grade Level.** Indicate the appropriate grade levels for this project.
- **Summary.** Briefly describe the project in one or two paragraphs. This paragraph should catch the interest of your readers. You can include a more detailed description later on in the call.
- **Number of Participants.** Indicate the number of classrooms or students that you wish to work with.
- **Project Coordinator.** Give your name and email address here. Be sure to fill out the contact information at the bottom.
- **Project Time Line.** Write out the time line for your project with specific dates. This should summarize the important steps of the project.
- **Complete Project Outline and Procedures.** Describe your project in greater detail. Be specific regarding what your responsibilities will be as well as those of the other teachers and students. This description should give participants a clear idea of what will be expected of them and should be a page or two in length depending upon the complexity of your project.
- **How to Register.** Provide complete information for registering for your project here. You may want to include all or some of the following information from potential participants:

Your full name	School voice phone
Your email address	Home voice phone
School/class Web address	Grade(s) taught
Your school name and address	Subject(s) taught
School district	

7. At least five weeks before the start date, post your first call for participation to the sites listed above. Repeat your call again two weeks before the start date. Enlist and train responsible students to be part of your project staff. This will be a big time saver!

8. At the project's conclusion, share the results of the project with all participants. Have your students write a summary of the project, including what they did and what they learned. Send a copy of this summary, along with project results, to your colleagues, principal, PTA president, superintendent, and board of education president. It makes for great district-wide Internet PR!

Internet Lesson Plan/Project Idea Sheet

Use this worksheet to rough out your Internet lesson plan and project ideas that are suitable for your students and curriculum.

Title: _____

Type: _____

Subject: _____ Grade Level: _____

Description: _____

Objectives — Your students will do/learn: _____

My educational/skill goals: _____

Materials: _____

Internet resources involved/addresses: _____

     URL: _____ URL: _____

     URL: _____ URL: _____

     URL: _____ URL: _____

Other resources: _____

Procedures: _____

Non-Internet activities: _____

Internet activities: _____

Set-up time required: _____

Class time required: _____

Problems/Issues that may be encountered: _____

Solutions/workarounds: _____

Assessment measures: _____

Follow-up activities/extensions: _____

Where to Post Calls for Project Participation

Classroom Connect Mailing List

mailto:crc-request@listserv.classroom.com

Type **subscribe digest crc** in the body of the message.

Electronic SchoolHouse Projects on AOL

America Online keyword: ESH

Global SchoolHouse Projects Registry

http://www.gsh.org/gsh/class/projsrch.html

GlobalWatch Internet Projects Mailing List

mailto:majordomo@gsn.org

Type **subscribe global-watch** in the body of your message.

HILITES Mailing List

mailto:majordomo@gsn.org

Type **subscribe hilites** in the body of your message.

IECC Projects Mailing List

http://www.stolaf.edu/network/iecc/iecc-projects.html
mailto:iecc-projects-request@stolaf.edu

Type **subscribe** in the body of your message.

IDEAS Project Posting Service

After you get your call for participation filled out and you're ready to post it to mailing lists, Usenet news-groups, and Web sites, send it to this address as well.

mailto:IDEAS@ACME.FRED.ORG

The staff of the Global SchoolNet Foundation will forward it to their international mailing lists for you. If you provide them with six to eight weeks lead time, they'll also re-post it for you again two weeks before the project begins. Be sure your call includes examples of the kinds of writing or data collection that students will submit.

HOW TO PLAY IT SAFE ONLINE

Educators worldwide know that bringing the Internet into the classroom promotes educational excellence and breathes new life and excitement into the educational experience.

However, educators and parents are justifiably concerned about the appropriateness of some material online. They're becoming aware that regulating how Internet connections are used in schools is almost as important as getting connected. Such concerns are understandable, but don't let them keep the Internet out of your school or stall your district's move to full Net connectivity. The Internet is just too valuable.

Concern About Content — Acceptable Use Policies

Most schools and districts that are already online have taken measures to keep inappropriate material out of the classroom. Hardware and software controls are often used to limit student and faculty access to certain Internet resources, such as specific Usenet newsgroups. Sometimes computers are available to students only by appointment and under strict supervision. Whatever the control strategy, there's no guarantee that a knowledgeable, determined user won't find a way to access inappropriate material or misuse his or her time on the Net.

To protect the school and reassure parents, administrators and technology coordinators must create and implement an Acceptable Use Policy, or AUP. An AUP is a written agreement signed by students, their parents, and teachers that outlines the terms and conditions of Internet use. It specifically outlines acceptable uses of the Internet, rules of online behavior, and access privileges. It also defines the penalties for violations of the policy, including security violations and vandalism of the system. Anyone using a school's Internet connection should be required to sign an AUP and know that it will be kept on file as a legal, binding document.

What Should Be Included in an AUP?

If your school district is just beginning to get online, your administrators and school solicitor may only now be learning of the existence of AUPs. You can save time and gain the benefit of other schools' experience by reviewing AUPs already in use. To give you an idea of what should be included in your school's AUP, here's a detailed rundown of an AUP's contents, along with sample wording.

1. **Begin with basics.** Explain what the Internet is, how students and teachers will access it, and how they'll use it in classrooms. Don't assume that parents know what the Internet is. Bring them up to speed with as little techno-jargon as possible, and be sure to cover all of the basics.

   Sample wording: "Internet access is now available to students and teachers in our school district. The access is offered as a collaborative project involving your student's school and a local Internet Service Provider. Our goal in providing this service is to promote educational excellence in the district by facilitating resource sharing, innovation, and communication.

   "Our connection provides direct access to the Internet, an 'electronic highway' connecting millions of computers and individuals all over the world. Your student will use it to communicate with fellow students all over the planet."

2. **Emphasize student responsibility.** Stress that students will be held responsible for their behavior while online. Explain that students will be taught about behavior that is not permissible on the network. Emphasize the importance of having the Internet in the classroom, but also make parents aware of the potential risks of students obtaining "objectionable" material. Be sure to mention the name and capabilities of special protection software, such as SurfWatch or CyberPatrol, that your school may use.

   Sample wording: "The smooth operation of the network relies upon the proper conduct of its users, who must adhere to strict guidelines. These guidelines are provided here so that you are aware of the responsibilities you are about to acquire. These responsibilities include respecting the privacy of other users, the right of all users to free expression, and crediting other users' works. With access to computers and people all over the world comes the availability of material that may not be considered of educational value in a school setting. We have taken precautions to restrict access to controversial materials by teaching students about responsible use and by using CyberPatrol software to block student access to inappropriate materials."

3. **List the penalties.** Emphasize that use of the Net is a privilege, not a right. Consider including a short paragraph about Internet etiquette, called netiquette, which users adhere to while online. Outline the penalties and repercussions of violating the AUP. Some schools issue a warning letter to students and parents after the first violation. Subsequent violations may result in students having their access restricted or being suspended from the system.

   Sample wording: "The use of our school district's Internet connection is a privilege, not a right. Inappropriate use will result in a cancellation of those privileges. Before receiving an Internet account and password, each student will meet with a faculty member to learn about proper use of the network, become familiar with netiquette, and review the AUP. The system administrators will deem what is inappropriate use, and their decision is final. The administration, faculty, and staff may request the system administrator to deny, revoke, or suspend specific user accounts."

4. **Sign on the dotted line.** Provide space for everyone to sign. Students should sign to show that they have read the document and understand its contents. Parents sign to verify that they're aware that there's a remote chance their student could access potentially inappropriate material, and that they accept responsibility if their child accesses your school's Internet connection from home. Teachers should sign on behalf of the school. Many schools host a "technology night" to introduce families to the Internet. Teachers meet with students and their parents to talk about how the Net will be used, to explain the AUP and its ramifications, and have all parties sign.

Do Your AUP Homework

Before creating your own AUP, take the time to see what other schools have done. Many schools across the country make copies of their AUPs available online. Use these as a template for creating your own, modifying as necessary to fit your particular needs.

- Boulder Valley School District's AUP is a great example of a successful AUP used at one of the United State's pioneering schools. For a copy, send an email message per the following directions.

    mailto:info@classroom.com

    Type **send aup-faq** in the body of your message.
- ERIC (Educational Resource and Information Center)

    http://ericir.syr.edu
- Armadillo's WWW Server

    http://www.rice.edu/armadillo/acceptable.html

When doing your AUP homework, take full advantage of Internet mailing lists and Usenet newsgroups to discuss your needs, ask questions, and talk with other educators who have successfully implemented AUPs at their schools.

- Consortium for School Networking mailing list

    mailto:listserv@listserv.net

    Type **subscribe cosndisc <Your Name>** in the body of the message.
- EDnet mailing list

    mailto:listproc@lists.umass.edu

    Type **subscribe ednet <Your Name>** in the body of the message.
- Usenet newsgroups

    news:alt.education.research

    news:misc.education

    news:k12.chat.teacher

Filtering Software

It can be difficult to supervise all of your students' Internet adventures. That's why many schools and families are relying on new, powerful software that blocks access to inappropriate sites.

Software products with such catchy names as Net Nanny, SurfWatch, and CyberPatrol are programs that parents and teachers can use to enter the Internet addresses of specific Internet sites they want to block or filter. In addition, the software usually comes with a list of sites that are already filtered out. Anyone trying to access areas designated as blocked is quickly thwarted, and students who wander around cyberspace will be less likely to stumble across inappropriate sites. Teachers, technology coordinators, or other adult administrators holding the passwords can still access whatever they wish, but children are effectively blocked from entering.

Since no parent or teacher can possibly keep up with all the inappropriate sites that spring up each week, these companies employ Net-savvy workers to constantly explore and add sites to their databases of restricted areas. Most of these products include access to these databases for no cost for the first several months, then charge subscription fees for users to stay current.

The features of these software packages vary. Some now block outgoing information, preventing users from sending out their phone numbers, addresses, and credit card numbers. Others even regulate access to computer games and other applications stored on your computer's hard drive, such as finance software or gradebook programs. These programs are supposedly "hack-proof," so that if anyone tries to tamper with the software settings, Internet access is totally blocked and the administrator is notified. Some of the programs even shut down the computer! Most are available in either single-computer or network versions, and nearly all offer steep discounts for educational organizations.

Not surprisingly, not everyone in the educational community is fond of blocking software. Some educators and administrators believe that such programs hamper children from learning how to deal with such material in a responsible, mature manner and will only make it more difficult for them when they confront such materials as adults. Others consider the programs a blatant form of censorship. Do these programs help educators better manage student access and select appropriate material? Or will schools misuse them, leading to an atmosphere of censorship and distrust? Who decides which sites should be blocked? These are questions that your school district should consider before buying this type of software.

Keep in mind that, although they are powerful and difficult to "hack," none of these filtering programs are completely foolproof. Installing one on a computer at home or school does not give adults the freedom to simply forget about the problem of inappropriate material. There is always a chance a youngster will stumble upon an inappropriate site or discover your password.

Where to Find Filtering Software

Bess.Net

206-971-1400
http://bess.net
mailto:bess@bess.net

CyberPatrol

Microsystems Software, Inc.
600 Worcester Road
Framingham, MA 01702
tel: (508) 416-1000
fax: (508) 626-8515
http://www.cyberpatrol.com
mailto:info@microsys.com

Net Nanny

Net Nanny Software International Inc.
525 Seymour Street, Suite 108
Vancouver, B.C. Canada, V6B 3H7
Phone: (604) 662-8522
Fax: (604) 662-8525
http://www.netnanny.com
mailto:netnanny@netnanny.com

SurfWatch

SurfWatch Software, Inc.
175 South San Antonio Road, Suite 102
Los Altos, California 94022
(800) 458-6600
http://www.surfwatch.com
mailto:info@surfwatch.com

ScreenDoor

Palisade Systems, Inc.
2501 North Loop Drive
Ames, IA 50010
(888) 325-6500
http://www.palisadesys.com
mailto:info@palisadesys.com

WebSense

NetPartners Internet Solutions, Inc.
9210 Sky Park Court, First Floor
San Diego, California 92123
Phone: (800) 723-1166, (619) 505-3020
Fax: (619) 495-1950
http://www.websense.com
mailto:sales@websense.com

Information Literacy

Thanks to the Internet, you and your students now have more information at your fingertips than at any other period in the history of the world. Once you're on the Net for a few weeks, you'll find yourself retrieving lots of online resources — from incredible photographs taken by the Hubble telescope, to breaking news stories your students will want to include in their class projects right away. However, this freely accessible repository of information poses some challenges to adult and student researchers alike.

Information Highway Potholes

Here's the main concern: On the Internet, anyone can publish anything to a worldwide audience in seconds. This "information" could read like an entry from a textbook but could contain inaccurate, unsubstantiated, or even misleading information. On the Net, in many cases, there are no "information gatekeepers." In the real world, only after a time-intensive process does a textbook, magazine, or feature article get published. But in cyberspace, gone are the professional editors and proofreaders who question, sometimes rewrite, but always check the validity of information in an author's work.

So as your students read and retrieve information from the Net to integrate into their schoolwork, how will they know that what they're reading is "good" information they can trust? The key is to teach yourself and your students how to sort the good online information from the bad. In short, you and your students need to become "information literate." Indeed, information literacy has become one of this year's hottest educational buzzwords — and for good reason.

How to Separate Good Information from Bad

The ability for anyone with a computer and modem to publish something on the Internet provides incredible opportunities for free expression and information sharing, but also offers the unscrupulous and irresponsible a global stage for their views. False, incomplete, or inaccurate medical, legal, and scientific information can be found on a variety of Web pages and Usenet newsgroups on the Net.

To make things even more complicated, many people use the Internet to post their political views or satirize public figures, events, and places. Parodic Web pages of Microsoft owner Bill Gates and the White House Web site have sprung up. At first glace, these sites could easily be mistaken for "official" Web sites, as they often mimic the page layout and even Net address of the original. The White House parody, for example, looks virtually identical to the real site. However, note the differences in the last three letters of these addresses.

http://www.whitehouse.net
http://www.whitehouse.gov

Which is the real site? Only after a close read of each home page is it evident that **www.whitehouse.gov** is the real one. If your students are unfamiliar with the concept of satire or are unfamiliar with the subject matter, they could simply accept what they read as accurate.

The key is to be a little critical about everything that's published online. Be sure to gather material from a variety of sources, including your Library Media Center. When you use Internet resources, be curious, ask questions, and examine related information, online and off.

Checklist for Evaluating Online Information

Here are some questions you and your students should ask as you evaluate the online information you uncover on the Internet.

- **What is the source of the information?** How can you tell whether you're reading information posted by an organization or by an individual user? Many times, a site's address will provide some clues. A legitimate information provider will have a straightforward online address, such as **http://www.xyz.com**. On the other hand, an individual user will have an online address reading something like **http://www.xyz.com/~sjm/data.html.** The **~sjm** part of the address gives it away. In this case, an individual with the initials SJM has put Web pages in his or her personal Web directory and made their contents available to the world.

- **Why is this information online?** If you know why the information is online, you'll be better prepared to assess its value. Think critically about the information. Is the purpose of the online information to inform and educate Internet users about a particular topic, or could there be a hidden agenda involved? Is the site sponsored by a group with a special, perhaps biased, interest in the topic?

- **Who wrote the information?** This is perhaps the most important question you need to answer about the information you find online. Material that's written by a known expert in his or her field is likely to be okay. If you've never heard of the author or the sponsoring organization, you should do more research into his or her background before accepting the information as factual. Go to an online engine and type in their name as your keywords.

Classroom Connect Search Page

http://www.connectedteacher.com/tips/tips.asp#se

What comes up? Do they seem to be highly knowledgeable about the topic? What else have they published? Check the library to see if this person has published anything else. Have they been known to write questionable things in the past on this same topic, online or off?

- **Does the online information contain links to other sites that reveal any biases of the author?** Following the links authors place inside their information is one of the best ways to discover more about the author and can reveal biases.

- **How recent is the information?** While new information is not necessarily any more accurate than old information, this is still an important question to answer. If you're doing a report on the current state of the former Soviet Union, you may want to steer clear of any information put online before 1991.

- **How often is the site/information updated?** This is a question you can usually answer by reading the home page of the site. Messages like "Last updated September 1, 1996" are prevalent on home pages across the Web. The creators of these sites know up-to-date information attracts users. If the site you're using as a source has no such message, look to see if anything else on the site is dated. If you can't find any, the site may not have been updated for a while.

- **How does this site compare with others that deal with the same subject matter?** You're sure to find several sources of online information that seem to be reliable and pass the scrutiny of the questions already posed above. As another check, search the Internet to see if other authors refer to the sources. If several do, chances are it's probably good information. Also, search for related documents to see how the authors' perspectives compare to one another. Don't forget traditional resources such as textbooks, journals, and other print materials in your media center!

Other Questions to Ask

- Who is the main audience for this information?
- Does the text follow basic rules of grammar, spelling, and literary composition?
- How knowledgeable is the individual or group on the subject matter of the site?
- Is contact information for the author or producer included in the document so you can email the person with questions or comments?
- What is the value of the Web site in comparison to the range of Library Media Center resources available on the topic you're researching?
- Does the author of the online information cite his or her sources in the document so you can check them for authenticity?

Becoming information literate takes time. But armed with this checklist of questions and a willingness to check your sources, you'll find that separating the "good" online information from the "bad" is a rewarding, enlightening experience.

Citing Internet Resources

Just as your students need to cite the books and periodicals they use to support their research, so too must they cite the online sources of information. With that in mind, we present a method to you for citing Net resources as accessed through your Internet browser. It will make it easy for you to check the truthfulness and accuracy of every online source your students cite.

Email

Structure

Author of email message. Subject line of the message. [Online] Available

email: Student@address.edu from Author@address.edu

date of document or download.

Example

Jones, Tom. Nile River Research Project results. [Online] Available

email: student5@smallvillehigh.edu from ert@informns.k12.mn.us

September 25, 1996.

World Wide Web

Structure

Author. Title of item. [Online] Available

http://address/filename

date of document or download.

Example

Yule, James. The Cold War Revisited: A Splintered Germany. [Online] Available

http://usa.coldwar.server.gov/index/cold.war/countries/former.soviet.block/Germany/
germany.html

November 5, 1996.

Telnet

Structure

Author. Title of item. [Online] Available

telnet://address, path

date of document or download.

Example

Jackson, Fred. Statistical Weather Data for Ohio, January 1996. [Online] Available

telnet://weather.machine.umich.edu,WeatherData/January1996/States/Zooms/Ohio

December 25, 1996.

Gopher

Structure

Author. Title of gopher item. [Online] Available

gopher://address/path

date of document or download.

Example

Kinyon, John. India: A Country in Transition. [Online] Available

gopher://gopher.india.gov:70/11/papers/trans

October 5, 1996.

Usenet Newsgroups

Structure

Author. Title of item. [Online] Available

news://group

date of document or download, if document is not available.

Example

Madige, Ellen. How to Build a Better Mousetrap. [Online] Available

news://sci.tech.inventions.mousetrap

January 16, 1996.

Online Image

Structure

Description or title of image. [Online Image] Available

http://address/filename

date of document or download if document is not available.

Example

Hubble Space Telescope release in the Space Shuttle's Payload Bay. [Online Image] Available

ftp://explorer.arc.nasa.gov/pub/SPACE/GIF/s31-04-015.gif

October 1, 1996.

Online Sound

Structure

Description or title of sound. [Online Sound] Available

http://address/filename

date of document or download, if document is not available.

Example

Reflections on Apollo. [Online Sound] Available

ftp://town.hall.org/radio/IMS/NASA/100394_nasa_01_ITR.au

September 25, 1996.

Online VideoClip

Structure

Description or title of videoclip. [Online VideoClip] Available

http://address/filename

date of document or download if document is not available.

Example

Shoemaker-Levy Comet enters Jupiter's atmosphere and breaks up. [Online VideoClip] Available

ftp://ftp.cribx1.ubordeaux.fr/astro/anim/sl9/breakingup.mpg

March 5, 1996.

Net Sites about Citations

Classroom Connect: How to Cite Internet Resources

http://www.connectedteacher.com/newsletter/citeintres.asp

Citing Electronic Documents

http://www.williams.edu:803/library/library.www/cite.html

Launch to Citing Online Addresses

http://www.pitsco.inter.net/p/cite.html

MLA Citation Guide

http://www.cas.usf.edu/english/walker/mla.html

APA Style of Notation

http://www.uvm.edu/~xli/reference/apa.html

Glossary

Acceptable Use Policy (AUP) A legally binding document signed by online users that regulates the rules of Internet use at a school, business, or home.

Boolean searching The process of adding the words *and, or, not,* or two parentheses, or an asterisk (*) between and around the keywords in your searches. These words and characters are known as Boolean operators.

Browser (See Web browser)

Commercial online service A company that, for a fee, allows computer users to dial in via modem to access its information and services, which now includes indirect access to the Internet. Examples are America Online and Prodigy.

Database A computer holding large amounts of information that can be searched by an Internet user. A storehouse of information on the Net.

Dialup Internet connection Lets a user dial into an Internet Service Provider using a modem and telephone line to access the Internet.

Directory A list of files or other directories on a computer at an Internet site.

Download/Upload To download is to transfer (retrieve) a file from another computer to the user's computer. To upload is to send a file to another computer.

Email Allows users to send and receive messages to each other over the Internet and through commercial online services like America Online and Prodigy.

Emoticons Smileys and other character art used to express feelings in email communication, such as :-).

Filter Hardware or software designed to restrict access to certain areas on the Internet.

Flame To send a harsh, critical email message to another user (usually someone who has violated the rules of netiquette) by **spamming**.

Frequently Asked Questions (FAQ) FAQ files answer Frequently Asked Questions on thousands of Internet-related topics. They're freely available at many locations on the Net. This ftp site holds every FAQ on the Net.

ftp://rtfm.mit.edu/pub/usenet/news.answers/

Graphical user interface Software designed to allow the user to execute commands by pointing and clicking on icons or text to navigate the Internet.

Hacker A computer user who illegally visits networked computers to look around or cause harm.

Home page The first Web page a user sees when visiting a World Wide Web site. Akin to a table of contents or main menu on a Web site.

Hotlist A personal list of favorite Web addresses organized in a single list. All Web browsers allow users to create hotlists so users can return to their favorite Web sites. Also known as Bookmarks.

HTML (Hypertext Markup Language) Programming language of the World Wide Web. HTML turns a text document into a hyperlinked World Wide Web page.

Hyperlink A highlighted word or graphic in a Web document that, when clicked upon, takes the user to a related piece of information on the Internet.

Hypertext The mechanism that allows Internet users to browse through information on the Web. Web pages are created with hypertext (HTML) and contain links to other Web documents or resources located on Internet computers.

Infobot (or mailbot) An email address that automatically returns information requested by the user. Akin to a real world faxback service.

Internaut Anyone who uses the Internet.

Internet The global "network of networks" that connects more than four million computers in 160 countries. The Internet is the virtual space in which users send and receive email, logon to remote computers (telnet), browse databases of information (gopher, World Wide Web), and send and receive programs (ftp) contained on these computers.

Internet account Purchased through an Internet service provider, the account assigns a password and email address to an individual or group.

Internet server A computer that stores data that can be accessed via the Internet.

Internet Service Provider (ISP) Any organization that provides access to the Internet. Many ISPs also offer technical assistance to schools that want to become Internet information providers by placing their school's information online. More information about ISPs can be found in Chapter 1.

Internet site A computer connected to the Internet containing information that can be accessed using an Internet navigation tool.

IP address Every computer on the Internet has a unique numerical address assigned to it, such as 123.456.78.9.

Keyword A word or group of words that can be searched through the Internet's search engines.

Logon To sign on to a computer system.

Mailing lists There are more than 4,000 topic-oriented, email-based discussion groups that can be read and posted to. Internet users subscribe to the lists they want to read and receive messages via email.

Menu A list of online information that leads to documents or other menus.

Modem An electronic device that attaches to a computer and links that computer to the online world via a phone line. Modems are available for any computer, can be internal or external, and come in several speeds, known as baud rates (bps). The higher the baud rate, the faster the modem. Most Internet service providers allow you to dial into their systems at 14,400 bps, 28,8000 bps, or 33,600 bps. Modems with 56,000 bps are also available and usable.

Netiquette The rules of conduct for Internet users. Violating netiquette could result in flaming or removal from a mailing list. Some service providers will even cancel a user's Internet account, denying him or her access to the Net if the violation is severe enough.

Net surfer Someone who navigates the Internet in search of information.

Netscape Available for both Mac and Windows, Netscape is the most powerful, easy-to-use Internet browser on the Internet. This software is already in use by thousands of schools worldwide and has become the de facto Web browser for millions of Internet users.

http://home.netscape.com/comprod/mirror/

Network A group of computers that are connected in some fashion. Most school networks are known as LANs, or Local Area Networks, because they are networks linking computers in one small area. The Internet could be referred to as a WAN, or a Wide Area Network, because it connects computers in more than one local area.

Online/Offline When you are logged onto a computer through your modem, you are said to be online. When you're using your computer but are not connected to a computer through your modem, you're said to be working offline.

Posts Email messages sent to a mailing list or Usenet newsgroup to be read by subscribers or others on the Internet.

Request for Comments (RFC) Online documents that have to do with technical standards for the Internet.

Search engine An Internet site that allows for keyword searching of online information. See Chapter 5 for reviews of many of the Net's current search engines.

Signature file Return address information such as name, phone number, and email address that users put at the bottom of email messages.

Telnet Allows users to access computers and their data at thousands of places around the world, most often at libraries, universities, and government agencies.

URL (Universal Resource Locator) The address and method used to locate a specific resource on the Internet. A URL beginning with http:// indicates that the site is a WWW resource and that a Web browser will access it. See Chapter 1 for complete information aout URLs.

Usenet newsgroups More than 13,000 topic-oriented message bases that can be read and posted to. Also called newsgroups.

Virtual A computer-generated environment.

Web browser (also known as Internet browser or browser) Software that allows computer users to access and navigate the contents of the Internet. Commercial online services like America Online and Prodigy have their own graphical Internet browsers. Most users who access the Internet directly use the Netscape Internet browser or the Microsoft Internet Explorer browser to get around online.

Web page A single Internet document containing information that can be accessed over the World Wide Web.

World Wide Web (WWW or Web) A revolutionary Internet browsing system that allows for point-and-click navigation of the Internet. The WWW is a spiderweb-like interconnection of millions of pieces of information located on computers around the world. Web documents use hypertext, which incorporates text and graphical links to other documents and files on Internet-connected computers.

Index

H

I

W